Rebuilding Pro-Life Nonviolence

By John Cavanaugh-O'Keefe and Elise Ketch

Rebuilding Pro-Life Nonviolence

by
John Cavanaugh-O'Keefe and Elise Ketch
a baby boomer with a past and a millennial with a future

The pro-life movement aims for a simple recognition that life begins at the beginning, not the middle, that all humans are people, and that we shouldn't kill tiny people. That's pretty simple! However, this simple proposal requires a whole new culture of life and civilization of self-sacrificial love and radical solidarity- a society rising from the dead. And building that new culture will require a massive distributed campaign of nonviolence, including civil disobedience.

ISBN: 9798337873350

© 2024 by John Cavanaugh-O'Keefe and Elise Ketch.

All rights reserved.

Dedicated to the five aborted children whose remains were discovered in Washington DC on the Day of the Unborn Child in 2022

Ángel
Holly
Phoenix
Christopher X
Harriet

The setting ...

> When Mary came to where Jesus was and saw him, she fell at his feet and said to him, "Lord, if you had been here, my brother would not have died."
>
> When Jesus saw her weeping and the Jews who had come with her weeping, he became perturbed and deeply troubled, and said, "Where have you laid him?" They said to him, "Sir, come and see." And Jesus wept. So the Jews said, "See how he loved him." But some of them said, "Could not the one who opened the eyes of the blind man have done something so that this man would not have died?" So Jesus, perturbed again, came to the tomb. It was a cave, and a stone lay across it.

the stench ...

> Jesus said, "Take away the stone." Martha, the dead man's sister, said to him, "Lord, by now there will be a stench; he has been dead for four days."
>
> Jesus said to her, "Did I not tell you that if you believe you will see the glory of God?" So they took away the stone. And Jesus raised his eyes and said, "Father, I thank you for hearing me. I know that you always hear me; but because of the crowd here I have said this, that they may believe that you sent me." And when he had said this, he cried out in a loud voice, "Lazarus, come out!"

... and the grin

> The dead man came out, tied hand and foot with burial bands, and his face was wrapped in a cloth. So Jesus said to them, "Untie him and let him go."
>
> – John 11: 32-44
>
> *The grin isn't in Scripture. But you tell me: did he grin?*

Contents

Introduction 9
Part One: The pro-life movement as a whole 17
    The current state of the movement 19
    Facing opposition intelligently 25
    To rebuild the whole movement 30
    To rebuild: first, a solid base of pregnancy aid 32
    To rebuild: second, education to change minds 41
    To rebuild: third, nonviolent action to change hearts 56
    To rebuild: fourth, political action to change laws 61
    The vision and internal unity of St. John Paul II 65
Part Two: Rebuilding Pro-life Nonviolence 83
    Nonviolence, explained 85
    Modeling constructive criticism 102
    Consistent ethic of hospitality 149
Conclusion 156

Introduction

This is a sketch, outlining a vision of a new pro-life movement, beginning with a commitment to a strategy of nonviolence, returning to the original intent of the pro-life movement: to protect all unborn children everywhere, and to support their mothers.

The old strategy to end abortion and protect unborn children and their mothers included three basic parts:

- direct support to mothers or couples in need,
- education leading to protective legislation, and
- a change in law to protect life from conception (fertilization) to a natural death

This educate-to-legislate plan sounds reasonable, but in fact this strategy hasn't ever reversed a massive and deeply entrenched social evil. The model that proponents of this strategy usually cite is the great work of William Wilberforce, who led the abolitionist movement in Britain. This model does not apply to our situation at all, because slavery was not a part of daily life within the nation itself. The *income* from the slave trade and from slavery itself was substantial and it came to Britain, but the actual inhuman practice was somewhere over there. There were some slaves in Britain, but few. The British decision to end the slave trade and then slavery itself did not alter life within the country. By contrast, abortion is a significant aspect of American life, everywhere amongst us. If you don't know a list of acquaintances who have had abortions, that's not because it doesn't happen in your social circle; rather, it's because they are hiding it from you, because they find you unpleasantly judgmental. Turning away from abortion would be a disruption in the domestic lives and plans and hopes of many close neighbors, not just in the operation of some far-distant plantations. The people who voted to end slavery were not voting for a change in their own lives.

Nor is the American abolitionist movement a model for pro-lifers. American slavery was ended by war, not by thundering moral arguments. So the model offered by American abolitionists includes a civil war. That war had about one and half million casualties including 600,000 deaths, out of a population of 30 million: that's about two percent of the nation killed and another three percent wounded. If we imitate that model today, it would cost about seven million deaths and ten million wounded. That's a fantastically bad model – even if it works, which also seems fantastic.

When people face the argument squarely, no one defends the educate-to-legislate model. It endures as the dominant plan of the movement *because people flatly refuse to examine it*. They don't see an alternative, and so they do the best they can, and courageously refuse to admit the possibility of permanent failure.

But we are not arguing that America and the world will never protect unborn children and make peace between generations. Rather, we are arguing that this vast change cannot be achieved by the old strategy, education which leads to legislation.

Some will promptly respond that they do not expect education and legislation to bring results without prayer; prayer, they say, will transform education and legislation. That's not total nonsense; but prayer includes listening to God, not just making requests of him. God speaks to us in and through the real world. And in the world of time and space, where we live, the educate-to-legislate strategy does not end massive and deeply entrenched social evils. Wars do, but let's not plan on that. And campaigns of nonviolence have been proven – in our time, by Gandhi and King and the Poles and the former satellites of the Soviet Union – to be as powerful and effective and transformative as war. Genuine prayer leads out of dead ends; it doesn't encourage obstinate determination to stay stuck.

We can and must discard the old strategy and begin the work of a campaign of nonviolence – praying and reflecting and studying and training and then acting with disciplined and self-sacrificial love.

People will not quickly abandon an established habit – or strategy. But can we face past failures honestly? The old strategy – half a century old now – has witnessed a steady loss of support. The 2022 pro-life victory in *Dobbs v. Jackson Women's Health Organization* – the reversal of *Roe v. Wade* – has not ended abortion in America; it has only made it possible for some states to ban abortion. That's not a bad thing, but it's not the end of abortion in America, not even close – and it is probably the high-water mark of the educate-to-legislate strategy. And this modest incremental step came at a very high price. The way we got the reversal was by attaching the whole pro-life movement tightly to the Trump wing of the Republican Party. In doing that, we participated in polarizing the country. But this strategy has a next step which is impossible in a polarized nation. The next step in the old strategy is to pass pro-life laws in every state legislature – which requires some help from the Democratic Party – and we can't get that help because we demonized and alienated them. So some states will ban abortion, and others will not – and so anyone anywhere in the nation can get an abortion if they are willing and able to travel a bit more than was necessary in years past. That's all we got from the old strategy, and it's all we're going to get without a massive change in the movement.

The old strategy did get *Roe v. Wade* reversed. But the way pro-lifers got that far was by a political effort that was – unnecessarily – polarizing and divisive. The *way* we got *Roe* reversed blocks the next step, for as far into the future as we can see. Be honest: that's a failure!

A new strategy should aim to change minds and hearts, and then change laws. We should:

- work carefully to study and understand and follow the teaching in the *Gospel of Life* and in the *Compendium of the Social Doctrine of the Church*
- emphasize the power of nonviolence rather than expecting too much from standard politics
- adopt a global approach rather than a national approach

- recover feminism as an ally against eugenics
- end the habit of denouncing our opponents and instead seek out areas of cooperation, such as ...
- protect pregnant and postpartum refugees, and
- rebuild a global consensus against coercive population control measures

We can protect the most vulnerable people in our midst, our unborn brothers and sisters. But to do so, we need new ways of thinking, new ways of imagining, and new ways of acting.

Perhaps the *Dobbs* decision will be an inflection point, and pro-lifers will stop to think about a new pro-life strategy going forward. What we do next cannot be an imitation of what we have done in the past 50 years. So perhaps – God willing – we will think about changes in our overall strategy.

So we offer a new approach – consistent with the clear and forceful teaching of the Catholic Church and rooted in a commitment to nonviolence.

What if I'm not Catholic?

JCOK: I should note carefully that in all her labors to build a "culture of life and civilization of love," the Catholic Church has worked hard to cooperate with other Christians and other theists, and indeed with all people of good will. But being ready to cooperate with other approaches, including a completely secular approach, is one thing; explaining and developing such an approach is another. I am ready to cooperate.

EK: I'll do my best to translate religious passages for secular accessibility. But the social justice model presented by the

Catholic Church is definitely insightful and useful; I encourage that everyone at least give it consideration.

We need more than just Catholics in the pro-life movement! We need non-Christians! We need secularists! We need atheists! That being said, a core tenant of nonviolence is developing a tenacious faith in something bigger than oneself. So, like an Alcoholics Anonymous meeting, we're going to ask you to pick a "higher power." (We know it sounds woo-woo, but please roll with it rather than rolling your eyes.) Here are some suggestions:

- God (whoever that is to you)
- transcendental Truth and Love
- connection to the collective human spirit
- identification with the universal struggle

When we make mentions of "God," interpret that to mean whatever higher power you've chosen. We're also going to mention and recommend sacred practices, which may be substituted with secular alternatives so you can still tap into their benefits. For example, replace basic prayer with mindfulness meditation or a mantra; the goal is to achieve a similar psychological effect. If we urge you to "pray on it," take time to "contemplate" it instead. For prayers of petition, try "manifesting": willing it to come into existence. Anyone can fast in action, but trust that it is contributing to a greater good. When we talk about "soul," think of moral fortitude. And cling to the belief that nonviolence will prevail in due course; whatever that means for you.

Hopefully with these modifications you'll be able to glean insights from religious passages, regardless of where you are on your (non-)spiritual journey. To all the nontraditional pro-lifers, of all kinds: we're glad you're here.

This book includes ideas about "rescues." What's that?

Simply put, a rescue is an action to protect a person in danger. More specifically, in this discussion, rescues consist of three elements: a nonviolent direct action intended to disrupt the cycle of abortion violence, and defiance of the status quo of the state under the law, and putting your body between a preborn person and an abortionist in an act of radical solidarity. In other words, if you've challenged a law by nonviolently putting your body on the line out of love for an unborn baby, then – Congratulations! You've done an abortion rescue.

The rescue movement began with sit-ins at abortion clinics. Then there was a national effort to establish pro-life nonviolent action – sit-ins – in every state. While we sat in the doors of abortion clinics, no one died. We linked our lives and freedom to the lives of children and true freedom of women. This nonviolent movement included a serious albeit small international outreach. The movement grew – from a few thousand activists to tens of thousands – with Operation Rescue. But the "rescue" movement set aside the previous commitment to nonviolence. Then its momentum was broken by the penalties in a new Federal law, the Freedom of Access to Clinic Entrances (FACE) Act.

Rescues continue today in many forms. The most common form is "opportunity rescue," in which rescuers enter an abortion facility to hand out roses tagged with pregnancy helplines and leave before the police are called. In a "rose rescue," rather than leave, the rescuers choose to stay and risk trespassing charges. In a "parking lot rescue," rescuers distribute literature among the vehicles in the private parking lot of an abortion facility. In a "truth team," a couple enters the facility and makes a theatrical display of deciding to leave. While less common due to the risk of FACE charges (and sometimes conspiracy), sit-in and blockade style rescues do still happen! In a "human shields rescue," rescuers perform a soft blockade – that is, they block entry to the abortion facility using only their bodies. In a "lock & block," rescuers construct a hard blockade augmented with chains and locks.

While rescues sometimes save lives, the point of a rescue is to offer the babies what may be the only act of selfless love they will ever receive before they are killed. By loving them, we foster an encounter with their humanity. Others witness them through the witness of our love. In this way, rescue rehumanizes the preborn.

This book was written by a baby boomer drawing on a pro-life past (identified below as *JCOK*) and a millennial planning a pro-life future (identified below as *EK*). We do not agree about everything; the book is full of major agreements and minor disagreements. We do agree that we want people above all to follow their consciences. Think critically, and take our words with a grain of salt. But remember: if you think that something we say is awful, the person you're attacking didn't say it; the other one did.

> *EK: That doesn't make sense.*
>
> *JCOK: Yes, it does.*
>
> *[pause]*
>
> *JCOK: On second thought, I agree:*
> *it doesn't make sense.*
>
> *EK: On second thought, I agree:*
> *it does.*

Part One: The pro-life movement as a whole

The pro-life movement needs an overhaul. Millions of faithful people have worked faithfully for decades to keep the basic idea clear: unborn children are our children, right from the beginning of their lives. And that beginning of a person's life is right at the beginning, not in the middle. And we shouldn't kill each other.

Still, to build a movement, we need the comprehensive vision of a prophet of our time, St. John Paul II, who spoke of a new "civilization of love and culture of life." And to get there, we need to understand and unleash a dynamic of social change, or social repentance – nonviolence.

The current state of the movement

So what's the state of the pro-life movement in the immediate aftermath of *Dobbs v. Jackson*? *Roe v. Wade* was overturned in 2022, and then state after state banned abortion. So are we, perhaps, in pretty good shape, with some exceptions?

Look at the exceptions.

Since the beginning of the pro-life movement, there have been debates about laws that provide for various exceptions. Should it be legal to abort a child who was conceived by rape or incest? Should it be legal to abort a child with detectable – and detected – disabilities? Should it be legal to abort a child if the pregnancy threatens the health of the mother; and if so, how do we define health? Pro-lifers have been divided over these questions for generations.

What's quite new is a debate throughout the movement about when in pregnancy to protect the child by banning abortion. Should it be at six weeks, which would ban about 95 percent of surgical abortions? Or at 16 weeks, which would ban less than five percent? No pro-lifer would have debated that in the two previous generations, but that question is unsettled in the tangle of post-*Dobbs* legislative proposals.

The battle to stop abortion and protect children and help conflicted parents by legislation has shifted the focus from national legislation to state-by-state legislation. But there is an unsolved obstacle looming in the background: no leader in the movement expects that pro-life legislation will pass in all 50 states. Pro-lifers may prevail in 35 states. What that means is that anyone anywhere in America who can travel can get an abortion. It's less convenient, and more expensive – and out of reach for some women* and couples in west Texas or in North Dakota. But for nearly every American, abortion will be available in America for the foreseeable future, regardless of the *Dobbs* decision.

EK: When I use the term "women" or she/her pronouns generally, I am referring to more people than just women who are females. Some intersex, transgender, nonbinary, and other queer-identifying folks are not female or are not women, and may experience pregnancy. I know there are terms, phrases, and pronouns that are more inclusive, but for the sake of simplicity, I'm going to use "women" to refer to all of these people at once.

JCOK: I may not understand this, but I will roll with it.

EK: As an LGBT+ person, I appreciate that.

So far, post-*Dobbs*, every time abortion has been on a ballot, submitted to a direct vote, we have lost. We have won battles in court and in legislatures, but not in the ballot box. If that pattern holds, there will be no state that provides protection for the unborn.

State-by-state legislation poses challenges, but right behind that is a far larger problem: even if every state in America were to pass protective laws, abortion would still be available outside America. The generation that launched the pro-life movement grew up in a time when about two percent of Americans traveled abroad annually; a national ban on abortion could be expected to prevent most abortions. Travel has changed dramatically since then, and the changes are relevant to us. Today, about 40 percent of Americans travel overseas annually, for fun. That means that abortion will be available to most Americans even if abortion is banned throughout the nation. The laws in Canada, Mexico, Britain, Sweden and elsewhere are critical for us. That's a change from the past, and pro-lifers have not begun to wrestle with this huge new challenge.

We are divided over the question of prosecuting mothers for abortion. This is catastrophically ignorant, and it's new. When *Roe v.* was decided in 1973, it overturned anti-abortion laws in 50 states and the District of Columbia, laws that had been written and passed in the 19th century. So there was a full century of experience, in every state, protecting unborn children by law. Not a single state – not one! – prosecuted women. In 1981, the last time that pro-lifers thought they were on the brink of restoring legal protection for the unborn, a charming and dignified pro-choice US Representative from New Jersey, Millicent Fenwick (the real-life model for Lacey Davenport in the "Doonesbury" comic strip), warned about exposing women to prosecution again. I [JCOK] contacted her, reporting for *National Right to Life News*, and asked her if she could name a single woman who had been prosecuted in the previous century in America. She was an honest opponent: she called me right back and apologized for her error. Women faced horrendous conditions with back-alley abortions; they feared prosecution. But in fact, she admitted, women were not prosecuted. I asked US Senator Tom Eagleton, who was the Democratic candidate for Vice President in 1980, about prosecuting women for abortion. He had prosecuted abortionists in Missouri before he was elected to the Senate. He explained that prosecutors could theoretically go after women, but never did – for several reasons but chiefly a practical one. To build a case, you needed the testimony of women to jail the abortionist or the testimony of the abortionist to jail women. So you could go after a woman who was involved once, under immense stress, often with a limited understanding of what was involved – OR you could go after the man who offered help but produced a dead child and (often) a depressed mom, who knew clearly what was going on, who was not under obvious and overwhelming personal stress, and who was going to abort over and over. For people with brains, this was never a complicated choice. Prosecutors always left the mothers alone and went after the abortionists – always, everywhere. But now, ignorant pro-lifers insist that justice for the child requires prison for the mother. And the pro-life movement is divided about this. There's stupid, damn stupid, and then this new division.

In body count, "medical" abortion has pretty well caught up with surgical abortion. Across the country and around the world, pills that produce an abortion without killing the mother are available and relatively inexpensive. Figuring out how to intercept death kits in the mail is tough. Stopping abortion when you know exactly where and when children are scheduled to die is hard;

intervening when you don't know where and when is vastly more complicated.

The line between contraception and abortion has always been a little blurry. IUDs that contain some copper are undeniably abortifacient. That is, they do not stop fertilization; they prevent implantation. Is it an "abortion" to kill an embryo in the first week of life, before the child develops a placenta and gets successfully attached inside to the mother's uterus? Copper-coated IUDs present a clear case, but other implants and injectibles are still hotly debated. And pro-lifers are not united regarding this common but tangled question of life and death. Most pro-lifers work hard to avoid the question altogether, and to stay focused on surgical abortion with a small but identifiable corpse at the end.

One of the complications of in vitro fertilization is that most providers try to grow more implantable embryos than they need, to save time when there's a failure. So many parents of children born by IVF have a small store of extras somewhere. Those unused extras are viable embryos – cryo-preserved kids. They are our brothers and sisters, trapped in concentration cans. To become adult humans, they just need some kindness (including human warmth) and sustenance and protection and time. They don't need any new ingredients to become human. This too is a challenge for pro-lifers, involving staggering numbers of human lives. And – this too is a problem that pro-lifers almost always want to avoid. Duck and run!

Human cloning is legal. It's not happening yet, but it is on the horizon. It is likely to come, with a commitment to avoid cloning human *adults*. Cloning will be for therapeutic purposes, to grow cells. Practitioners will bring humans to life, planning at the outset to kill them – a deliberate policy of "clone and kill." Pro-lifers started fighting to ban human cloning, but abandoned the effort because it was complicated and not good for fundraising.

Pro-lifers face a list of challenges in a culture of death. But also, we have created a problem of our own. One branch of the movement, the activists on the streets, is divided about nonviolence. In the 1980s, the rescue movement grew rapidly, leading to tens of thousands of nonviolent actions to save lives. That growth depended in part on the support of pro-life leaders like Cardinal John O'Connor of New York. Rescue leaders visited him repeatedly, and he offered them his support repeatedly, but only after he asked for and got commitments to nonviolence – repeatedly. But by 1990, many leaders of the rescue movement had turned away from that guarantee. They argued that we shouldn't follow a pagan (Gandhi) nor a philanderer (MLK); we should instead follow "Biblical principles." Their "Biblical principles" included some ideas from 1 Samuel 15, in which God seems to demand that Saul slaughter all his enemies without mercy. In one deft improvement, these pro-life leaders moved from the Sermon on the Mount to genocide. That was divisive.

Politically, the national leadership of the movement has moved steadily to the right. We are now pretty well cleansed of all taints of liberal leftie loonies, including the horrible Demoncrats. That too is divisive. It's not possible to denounce that many people and keep building an effective movement.

So we're doing fine except that ...

1. the old exceptions are all still debated, unsettled – rape, incest, naked eugenics, and mother's health;
2. we debate amongst ourselves over a ban at six vs. sixteen weeks;
3. state bans are possible in 25-35 states, but not all 50;
4. every time abortion is on a ballot, we lose;
5. overseas abortions demand a global response;
6. we are divided over prosecuting mothers;
7. medical abortion is a growing challenge;
8. we are dodging problems with IUDs and injectibles and implants;
9. we have no plan to protect and cherish cryopreserved kids (IVF spares);
10. human cloning is legal;

11. some of us have discarded nonviolence and chosen "Biblical principles" like genocide;
12. we have rejected allies we need, because we have habits of division without habits of reconciliation.

The pro-life movement today is small and getting smaller, divided, without a plan. "God is on our side and we will be faithful": that's not a plan. There's still plenty of happy talk available, but it's not attached to reality.

Facing opposition intelligently

Besides the 12 new problems that have emerged in the past 50 years, there are four more huge challenges that we never faced squarely: snobbery, eugenics, legitimate loyalty to friends run amok, and admirable empathy for the abandoned run amok.

In the history of humanity, there has been nothing to compare with the abortion catastrophe of the 20th and 21st centuries. For decade after decade, about one child in four is killed, usually with the tacit agreement of the parents. Clear and reliable statistics about abortion rates don't exist, even in developed nations; but the total death toll since abortion took hold globally in the 1960s and 1970s is in the billions. The only way to exceed or even match that grim rate is by launching an all-out nuclear war.

Focusing on the United States (because it's familiar): why does anyone participate in this? Why do women and couples opt for abortion? Are there problems that need to be solved to end the bloodshed?

Answering that question carefully and definitively would require years of hard work and study, a small library of research. This short book doesn't do that; but we do want to raise the question, because our experience suggests that pro-lifers are rarely engaged in a thoughtful effort to figure it out. Our experience points to at least four reasons for promoting or accepting abortion that our pro-life colleagues often ignore completely. And obviously, an effort to build or re-build an effective pro-life movement needs a theory of what we are up against. And it's just nonsense to say we're struggling against feminism or choice or Communism or Satanic Democrats.

One major reason that many people adopt a pro-choice stance is utterly simple: "it's the right and proper thing to do." There's immense social pressure to be pro-choice – or perhaps more precisely, to avoid being a bleeping dirtbag like those anti-choice fascist nutcases over there. Don't be one of "them." That's not a logical argument, but it is very persuasive.

Years ago, I [JCOK] spent several months ghost-writing the autobiography of a very wealthy man – we'll call him "Jim" for now – and I learned a great deal from him (although we abandoned the book). At one point in his career, he decided to take his company public, to sell stock in it. The process was complicated, and a prominent New Yorker – Augie – befriended Jim and coached him through the process. There were business and banking decisions to make, but there was also a very serious socialization process. Augie expert coached Jim to fix his speech – for example, to say "ask" not "aks." And there were manners – about posture and neckties and such. In passing on those valuable lessons in culture to me, Jim added one that he had already intuited before he met his New York high society tutor: don't be an anti-choice fanatic. It's bad for business. Well, that was an interesting bit of advice: stand straight, fix your tie, and abandon the helpless. It's not logical, but peer pressure works.

It seems to me that there's another extraordinarily potent argument for abortion that is rarely challenged. Behind abortion, there are unstated assumptions taken from eugenics. Eugenics is a pseudo-science that became an influential ideology in the late 19th century. The idea is, we breed living things to improve them from one generation to the next. We breed roses and horses and tomatoes, all kinds of things – so of course we should breed humans, to get a better human race. Eu-genics: good genes. The eugenics movement brought forward several key ideas in the 1920s, including:

- they passed laws against "miscegenation," marriages between whites and other "races";
- they passed laws permitting or mandating the sterilization of "feeble-minded" people;
- they passed laws restricting immigration of inferior and stupid people, notably Jews and Chinese.

Their ideas about inter-racial marriage and about forced sterilization have been largely discarded, but their ideas about immigration persist.

A key notion behind their pseudo-science is that the life of an individual and the life of the whole human race evolve in similar ways. That is, life emerged from the slime and passed through various stages – one-celled creatures, amoeba, vertebrates, mammals, humanoids, blacks, then the pinnacle of development with whites. Similarly, an individual's life goes through stages: zygote to blastocyst to embryo to fetus to baby to adult. Stated pompously: "Ontogeny recapitulates phylogeny." This is lunatic science and a destructive ideology, but some scraps of this core idea from eugenics persist in abortion.

Pro-lifers ask, "When does life begin?" That question generally leads nowhere; pro-lifers are smug in their certainty that the beginning is the beginning while their opponents think the question is nonsense. Pro-choicers dismiss this the pro-lifers' question confident that life doesn't begin in a sharp and defined moment; instead, it slips-slides from one stage to the next, steadily collecting size and complexity and value. An individual begins as something like an amoeba, nearly valueless, and develops gradually to an adult, with the value we give any human.

That's eugenics. And that, not feminism, is the opposite of a pro-life stance.

One problem with that persistent slice of eugenic thought is that if an individual's life accretes value gradually, from zero to 100%, it must pass through *three-fifths* of human at some stage. And when an American notices that we are thinking about an entity that's three-fifths of a human, we might worry. America fought a Civil War to get rid of that pernicious idea, to remove it from the Constitution.

Similarly, eugenic thought requires that *we decide* when we will attribute full humanity, with all human rights, to the slowly developing thing – embryo, fetus, baby, whatever it is. And that decision by society puts us back into the business of having the State – not God, nor any other un-named source of self-evident truths – grant rights. Again, this is a matter about which Americans fought a war, to assert that we hold it to be self-evident that all people are created equal and endowed by their creator with rights. At his inauguration, John Kennedy raised the question again. He spoke of a torch passed to a new generation, and that torch was specific – the revolutionary belief that "the rights of man come not from the generosity of the state but from the hand of God."

Note well: this alternative belief, that the rights of man are created and conferred by social consensus, at some arbitrary point between conception and birth (rather than recognized in the simple fact of shared humanity) is brought to us by eugenics, and it is catastrophically contra-Revolution.

Pro-life education should prepare us to answer eugenics, a serious and murderous opponent – not to squabble with feminists, who were our natural allies in the past and will be again in the future.

A third argument for abortion, or cause for adopting a pro-abortion stance with or without argument, is simple loyalty. Loyalty is not the greatest virtue, but it's up there near the top. Many good people who experience sexual trauma themselves, or see others go through it, will make a decision with fiery determination to stand with the victims and support them in the decisions they make to escape. Often, escape from an abuser includes or involves abortion, ridding oneself of the residue of the assault.

A fourth reason for adopting a pro-abortion stance is a thoughtful and loving decision made by good people who choose empathetic identification with women dealing with abandonment. Offering support for a woman who trusted the wrong man and ended up pregnant and alone is laudable, not despicable. Standing with pregnant parents who feel isolated by complications is admirable, not detestable. And again, this loyalty leads many people to support abortion.

Killing a child is not a solution; it's another problem, worse than the first. But pro-life education should include a deep respect for the genuine virtues that may be intermingled in a pro-abortion stance. Pro-lifers who distort and demean their opponents' ideas cannot succeed in convincing anyone to choose life.

Too often, pro-life arguments are really just comfort food exchanged among pro-lifers, with no serious intent to challenge or change the prevailing culture. In the struggle to convince and convert, we must engage intelligently and respectfully!

The pro-life movement has a dozen problems that are new since 1973 and has four more immense challenges that are old but remain urgent and largely unaddressed. We need to rebuild the movement. There are millions of people who see clearly that unborn children are members of the human family, with all the rights of any human; but we are not yet organized to build a new protective civilization.

To rebuild the whole movement

The old movement had three parts: pregnancy aid and education and political/legislative initiatives. Pregnancy aid is to help women and couples one by one, directly; it is not an effort to transform society. The educational outreach had a clear aim, to prepare the way for laws that protect the unborn. And the legislative effort was the goal of the movement.

That cannot work. Yes, for sure at some time in the future we will have laws that protect the unborn. But laws reflect the society that writes them. If they don't embody the values of the people, they will be re-written, sooner or later. At this time, we do not live in a pro-life society. Perhaps we remember when we were a pro-life society; but right now, Americans generally accept abortion. There are millions of us who are completely convinced that unborn children are our brothers and sisters, but we do not speak for America (let alone for the whole world).

The new movement must be built to change hearts, aiming for a new culture of life and a new civilization of love. To get from here to there, we need a sustained campaign of nonviolence. We intend to change minds and laws, both – but changing hearts is primary.

As Christians understand it, changing hearts is the work of God, and so some people are adamant that we should pray and educate our own children. True, yes, great, do it – but no, absolutely no, that is not enough! Most pro-lifers are prepared to say that marriage is a call to "co-create," to work with God to create eternal beings. So to say that a critical task is the work of God does not in any way diminish our responsibility to get at it!

For everyone (that is, not just Christians), changing hearts is a matter of tapping into human instinct and the collective unconscious. Education teaches others to know rationally that abortion is wrong, but it will not move them to action until they reach this understanding on their own, deeper than rationality, in their non-rational minds. However, we can create subjective encounters that facilitate the formation of these intuitive connections. Just because this critical task is indirect does not diminish our responsibility to take direct action. After all, actions do speak louder than words.

We are called to engage in this work of changing hearts intelligently and proactively. The work of Gandhi, King, St. John Paul II and Lech Walesa and others in the 20th century proved beyond reasonable doubt that we can change the heart of a society as well as of individuals.

To change hearts: the heart of that effort is nonviolence. The new movement must include pregnancy aid, and education (including the theory and practice of nonviolence), and an autonomously organized and sustained campaign of distributed and direct nonviolent action. The goal is to build a society that loves and cherishes unborn people. That society will indeed write new laws, but the goal – and the way there – is self-sacrificial love for and radical solidarity with the most vulnerable people among us.

To rebuild: first, a solid base of pregnancy aid

Pro-lifers are justifiably proud of how much we have done to offer pregnancy aid.

Pregnancy aid is conceptually simple: here's a person feeling trapped, so figure it out and help. Someone tiny depends on her, and she is really truly not ready for that, but no one else can take over the whole responsibility. So it's huge, and it's sudden: go help.

Pray a lot, line up docs and lawyers and counselors, pray some more, plan how to talk to irate parents (who are grandparents too, all of a sudden), endure cars passing with a smattering of beep-beep-bleep, find emergency housing, protect her job, find some housing and employment, get a protective order, keep praying, meet boyfriend wants to kill someone maybe her or maybe you or maybe both, hussle, gotta live your own life too but she's in an emergency and a child's life is in the balance, angst and prayer and a list of emergency contacts and hussle – and oh by the way your neighbors think you're a bleeding bleeping GDSOB busybody who belongs in jail. Pregnancy aid is hours of boredom with violence and tension close by, 98 percent failure, up-to-date insults, and occasional success that – when it is achieved – properly belongs to someone else.

A part of the challenge in pregnancy aid is that fathers can walk away, apparently intact and often apparently untroubled. If a pregnant woman wants the same impunity that a man carries off so easily, she needs an abortion. If he can stroll away, why can't she? So faced with this glaring imbalance and injustice, whose side are you on?

A common problem – often obscured behind shame – is that the guy is abusive. Whose side are you on? This pregnancy is a "gift" from a violent and irresponsible male: whose side are you on?

In the century before *Roe v. Wade*, pro-lifers were accused of abusing women, and/or supporting men in the oppression of women. In fact, women were never prosecuted for abortion in the US, but the fear was real, one more complication in the abortion debate. And today, since the *Dobbs* decision, some pro-lifers are in fact working hard to jail women who get an abortion – not in nightmares, but in reality. Whose side are you on?

The most prominent "pro-life" politician in America today immediately post-*Dobbs* is Donald Trump. To many pro-lifers, he's a hero. People ask whether he is sincere, but he appointed three Supreme Court Justices, who reversed *Roe v. Wade*, so what else do we want? But there are many problems with this situation, including that he's been found by two juries to have abused – and possibly raped, depending on how you define the word – at least one woman. He said he could grab women's genitals if he wanted to, and he has acted on this obscene and brutal idea. This is the worst part of male chauvinism – and it shows up in a much-admired "pro-life" leader. That looms in the background when a pro-lifer offers help to a pregnant stranger: are you okay with men assaulting women? Whose side are you on?

So pregnancy aid is tough! But we do it anyway, because life is precious and peace is possible. We have seen children live and parents rejoice.

On one hand, it is tough, and so a critique of pregnancy must begin with respect for the great people who plunge in and help! On the other hand, there are some systemic failures we cannot overlook.

Today, the limitations and problems with our work in pregnancy aid are staggering. For me, the most painful shortcoming is the flat and fiery refusal to offer pregnancy aid to refugees. The pro-life movement has tied itself tightly to jingoist isolationists who are committed to a *national* movement and completely resistant to a *global* approach. If we were willing to love our enemies as nonviolence (and the Lord) demands, and listen to them respectfully, we might notice that the Biden administration already recognizes pregnant and postpartum refugees as a special class, a significant category that requires special assistance. So it is completely reasonable, not far-fetched, to urge this Democratic administration to provide pregnancy aid. Yes, we will have to compete a bit with Planned Parenthood, but we can build a program in which we provide millions or billions of dollars to help pregnant refugees. Here's a rough estimate of the opportunity regarding pregnant refugees, way over a million women annually: about a third of pregnant refugees will get abortions no matter what anyone else says, and a third will give birth no matter what anyone else says, and a third will make their decisions about life or death based on the hope and help offered by others. But they are multi-colored foreigners, and so the American pro-life movement *will not help them*. God have mercy on us! We are so completely gutted out!

EK: We have at least a few modern global connections. Pro-Life Global is an organization founded to address the 99% of abortions that happen outside the US; Progressive Anti-Abortion Uprising did a European tour, winning admirers and enemies; Rehumanize International has hired writers around the globe.

> JCOK: Very, very good – but not enough on its own. We need a movement-wide effort of global outreach.

I [JCOK] am a Catholic. When I was in grade school, I was taught by Holy Cross nuns, and I learned a "Morning Offering" that I have said (often, not daily) for about 67 years. "O Jesus, through the Immaculate Heart of Mary, I offer you all my prayers, works, joys, and sufferings of this day, for all the intentions of Thy Sacred Heart, in union with the holy sacrifice of the Mass throughout the world, in reparation for my sins, for the intentions of all of our associates, for the reunion of Christendom, and in particular for the special intention recommended this month by the Holy Father." In the version that I learned, we prayed in particular *for the intentions recommended by the Pope*. Throughout my life, my prayer and my support of the Pope have been completely intermingled. I don't pray alone, don't even know what it might mean to pray alone; I pray with – or at least I intend to pray with – angels and saints and the whole Church that the Lord founded. And the Pope serves this Church as a focal point and source of unity. I understand that Protestants don't pay much attention to the guy in a funny white dress in Rome, except maybe once in a while to denounce him; and that casual dismissal doesn't bother me much, because Protestants don't pretend to pray with the whole church around the whole world throughout all the centuries of Christianity. As I see it, Jesus prayed for all of us, so I try to go along with his prayer as well as I understand it, and I expect that one day the Church will be united and do the same – but not today. I say this to draw a contrast and offer a challenge (to Catholics). I pray with the Pope – unlike a whole boatload of Catholic leaders today, who feel free to dismiss his teaching and leadership, including his insistent plea that we pray and think globally, not just nationally or locally or individually. And I think his global perspective is a challenge for pregnancy aid – a challenge that we have failed to meet.

Church teaching about nationality is cautious. On one hand, patriotism is a great virtue, embraced and supported by the Church. On the other hand, an excessive nationalism can undercut catholicism; so the Church notes that it can be hard, in some cases, to distinguish between nationalism and racism. It seems to me that pregnancy aid is not racist *locally*; but *globally*, pregnancy aid is indeed racist, albeit blandly and blindly.

Of course, pregnancy aid is local, almost always, by design and function. We help women and couples one by one, face to face, heart to heart: that's got to be local. But networks of pregnancy aid matter; and these networks have their antennae up for pro-life issues beyond immediate service one by one. Where are there holes in the network? How can we do better on college campuses? Can we expand our use of sonography? Et cetera. The problem is, that antennae network is almost always national, not even trying to go beyond five percent of the world. Yes, there are occasional interesting contacts beyond our borders, to Ireland and Hungary and elsewhere, or perhaps attached to various mission activities. But do we have serious intentional programs? Nah, no way! Can we even decide to help pregnant refugees right at the border? Destiny Herndon de la Rosa does. Houston Catholic Worker does. Fr. Rick Thomas in El Paso did. But pro-lifers in general? No!

EK: Back up. You said pregnancy aid isn't racist locally, and I want to challenge that. Generally, pregnancy resource centers (PRCs) recruit outside of the communities they serve, which results in class and race disparities between the aid workers and the pregnant community members.

JCOK: Okay, I acknowledge this.

EK: So because the predominant model for pregnancy aid is based in charity, it suffers from systemic issues of classism and racism. The charity model sets up a hierarchical patron-client relationship of power, which enables infantilization and coercion. It's plagued by "white saviorism."

JCOK: What would you want to see?

EK: I think we need a solidarity model. In mutual aid, the service is directed by members of the community, and the community members being served have the opportunity to give back. This bilateral flow of aid distributes power horizontally and bridges the disconnect of the charity model, which hands out (or refuses) aid unilaterally.

JCOK: I support your view, and accept the challenge.

EK: And don't get me started on PRCs coercing mothers to give up their babies for the predatory domestic infant adoption industry to sell. Adoption is family separation, and that is the second-worst option. We can't let PRC networks gatekeep who gets to parent, as they will inevitably privilege some communities and marginalize others. We should prioritize family preservation, on the border and in pregnancy aid.

JCOK: We could – and perhaps should – write another book about that. But lets finish the thought about a global perspective ...

Pregnancy aid offers hope that life is possible, and Planned Parenthood doesn't offer that. But pregnancy aid groups also offer concrete support – diapers, medical care, housing, the whole array of human services. But Planned Parenthood, by contrast, supports a liberal agenda in which the whole community – on various levels of organization – offers perhaps ten times ten times ten times as much practical aid as we offer. Planned Parenthood supports liberal programs including universal health care, education for immigrants through college, housing, food aid ...

EK: Sure, Planned Parenthood supports practical aid in word, but outside of funneling cash to political campaigns that fit their agenda, do they offer even a facsimile of a contribution to them?

JCOK: I understand your point, but I think we should look more carefully at tax-supported aid programs. In ages past, people in need got help from family and neighbors, from the local community, and from religious organizations. But today, we are much more aware of needs that cannot be met by a local response. Education in the segregated South was not about to be fixed by generous local teachers; a proper response required Federal intervention. Plague and famine and war can't be ended by a local response, nor even a national response; we need an organized regional or even global response. Subsidiarity matters – problems should be handled by the smallest and most personal and local social unit that is capable of an effective response. But sometimes, the smallest effective unit is the globe. Many conservatives are fiercely resistant to international authority of any kind. And of course, in 2021, the insurrection at the U.S. Capitol featured Confederate flags parading through – symbols of resistance to excessive Federal authority. And some conservatives identify themselves a "conservative" meaning specifically that they resist many claims of authority made by large governmental entities.

I think that health care and education and housing and peace and justice require some support from national and global authorities – but that idea is a divisive among pro-lifers. To meet some human needs, we have to push hard against conservatives. And in those contests, I'm glad to find allies, even among people whose personal budget for charity – aside from taxes – might be skimpy.

EK: *Never forget, they are a capitalist corporation. If they didn't see profit in vocally supporting these programs, they'd be silent.*

JCOK: *Well, I won't work hard to defend Planned Parenthood; they are up there with Hitler and Stalin when measured by the number of dead bodies they produced. But I do know and respect many generous individuals who work for the abortion industry, including Planned Parenthood. Let me give a single example – not perfect but perhaps helpful. Around 1985, I was arrested with Alan Woll and Elsie Lewis at the Planned Parenthood clinic in Silver Spring, Maryland. We were inside, babysitting the suction machine. As long as we were there, nobody would die. The acting clinic administrator that day was Debbie Y--. She called the police and had us arrested. But we had to wait a while for transportation. So there we were, lying on the floor, handcuffed. It wasn't bad, but it looked awkward – so Debbie went and got me a pillow for my head. I didn't need it, but that was a kind gesture. Her work that day was to end the lives of some children; but that's not the way she understood it. She was, it seemed, habitually kind – to women and to strangers, including troublesome strangers. Like millions of people, she dismissed the claims made by tiny people, and I have spent a large part of my life upholding those claims; but I was privileged to get a glimpse of what made her tick. That pillow was not a big deal; it was nearly invisible next to the real issues of that day. But it was a kind gesture, from the heart, to a trespasser. Since that day, I have prayed – not every day but probably every month – that I would be like her, in some ways. I haven't seen her since except briefly in court; I wouldn't recognize her. But Debbie remains an inspiration to me.*

... But most pro-lifers, including many people who have devoted their lives to offering pregnancy aid, denounce all that practical aid as "Socialism." This is so ignorant, so nasty – and so anti-Catholic!

Pregnancy aid is a generous and praiseworthy activity, a whole list of works of mercy. But often, these works of mercy go hand in hand with fiery resistance to works of justice. This savage inconsistency is so god-awful.

When the government owns or controls the means of production, that's Socialism and it's a serious problem. When the government supports and funds social services, that's Catholicism, and it's a great blessing. This is not complicated.

EK: Okay, I'm anti-capitalist, and I know pro-life socialists.

> *JCOK: That's great! So do I! The word "socialist" doesn't mean what it meant a century ago, when Pope Pius IX condemned a list of things. But, Elise, are we gonna make it to the end of this chapter?*

EK: I just want socialists to know they are welcome in the movement too! Sorry, I'll quit interrupting for now.

A generous spirit is not a substitute for intelligence. It may be more important, but it's not a substitute. We are supposed to love God and neighbor with our whole heart and soul and strength – *and mind*. For Christians, we must follow the Lord and his Church, thinking and acting locally *and globally*, being proactive about helping pregnant and nursing moms everywhere we find them in dire need, working to provide the whole panoply of health and human services as a matter of justice. (EK: Ahem: for non-Christians and everyone else as well, this is a good model to follow.)

To be crystal clear: pregnancy aid is the beginning of pro-life work; it is foundational, and indispensable. However, immediately post-*Dobbs*, American pregnancy aid generally displays two crippling systemic problems: it is appropriately local but inexcusably resistant to a global perspective, and it is often inexplicably resistant to cooperating with government agencies to provide extensive health and human services.

To rebuild: second, education to change minds

The basic education is the same now as in 1973: following the lead of Jack Willke, we need to explain carefully, with photos, what conception and growth up to birth looks like, and what abortion looks like.

Pro-lifers assert that the beginning of life is at the beginning, not in the middle. It's ridiculous to say it begins at 12 weeks or 16 weeks. 12 weeks after what? After the beginning. The beginning is right at the beginning, and any other answer is absurd.

However, pro-lifers make several assumptions that need to be stated clearly and debated openly. We assert that the beginning is at the beginning. But we assume without debate that there is a beginning, that life is not a continuum. We assume that the life of an individual is significant, not just the life of a society. We assume that the beginning is objective and discernible, not arbitrary and obscure. To us, these assumptions seem obvious; that's why we assume them. But they are *not* obvious, and they are *not* accepted universally. We need open debate about them. And this debate is not about *when* a new life begins, but *whether*. Is there a beginning, or are we faced with slight alterations along a smooth continuum? This is the real debate, and it is about eugenics, which does not see or accept creative and decisive and even explosive moments of creation.

Philosophy

Pro-life leader (and atheist) Terrisa Bukovinac wrote, "We must be able to confidently ground our pro-life conclusions in moral philosophy using a secular and shared basis of understanding. Our credibility relies on this foundation." Most pro-lifers can explain why a new life begins biologically at fertilization, but have never been taught to explain how personhood begins ontologically then too! Spreading a solid account of personhood based in process philosophy a la Kristina Artuković could change that.

So how are preborn humans actual, not potential, people? Well, every person is attaining, retaining, or reattaining the best version of themself, including you, right? This is an active process people go through called "enselfment."

Picture a specific being that is their best self, then imagine when that being first began to exist as a distinct whole individual. That whole being at their beginning is the same whole being that became the best self, which means there is an active and inherent relation between the best self and the beginning whole being. The whole being from the beginning was becoming the best self – but, a being can't become a best self before they are a self. That must necessarily mean that the whole being at the beginning was already a self, so the very first version of that particular self existed when the whole being began to exist.

The process of enselfment is inherent to the nature of humankind, so all members of the human family are actively "enselfing" as long as they are alive. If every being that is a version of a self is a person, and all living humans are enselfing, then all living humans must become people when they begin to exist as whole beings. At fertilization, a human embryo becomes a whole organism – she is complete and does not lack anything essential to herself, she only requires sustenance and time to become her best self, so she is already a self. How neat is that!

The very first version of the self of a human begins to exist at fertilization when they become a whole being, so all humans start to be people at fertilization. Your being was contingently incapable at the beginning of your life, but was actively and inherently enselfing, meaning your early life form was the selfsame person that you are now. The preborn are integrated physically by development and metaphysically by active relation with the person they will later manifest, so they already are that person latently.

When we skip the step of explaining "how" the preborn are people before detailing "why" they are, we leave a huge hole in our pro-life accounts of personhood. It's a disservice to unlink the physical facts from our metaphysical reality.

Miniaturization

It is one of the puzzles and painful ironies of our time that abortion has expanded even as technology made it easier and easier to see and understand what tiny humans do. The rhythm of life, the heart-throb that signals life and sometimes signals love, begins before we have a fully-developed heart. At just 21 days after fertilization, our primitive hearts begin to beat, pulsing blood through our bodies. Who knew that a century ago?

There was a debate in the Middle Ages about the interface between the physical universe and other realities – angels or spirits or extra-terrestrial creatures who dwell in other dimensions. One question that they asked was, "How many angels can dance on the head of a pin?" It's odd today to watch intelligent people who are proud of their open and flexible minds deal with the medieval question. Often, modern and secular thinkers laugh at the stupid question. And then, perhaps the following week but perhaps the next minute, they reveal that it's obvious that a human body can't have a human soul until it weighs about a pound (which is too big for even one to dance on the head of a pin). That is, they laugh at the stupid question, then answer it in a slightly altered format, and their answer is ridiculous.

If I can put a thousand books on my phone in my pocket, why is it hard to imagine that a miniature human might have immense capabilities? Babies grow fingers: that's astounding. Mom doesn't make the fingers and attach them; babies do it by themselves. Their little body-minds are fantastically creative!

But surely a tiny zygote can't have a mind. They don't even have a brain! What is a body-mind, anyhow?

For Reber, Baluska, and Miller, "life and consciousness are coterminous." According to their theory of the Cellular Basis of Consciousness, even cells – minimal units of life – have minimal consciousness. Dr. Thomas Verny wrote that "before the event of birth, before we have even had a glimmer of sight or sound in the womb, we record the experience and history of our lives in our cells," and coined this process "bodywide memory." As an embryo, intrauterine stressors upon your body sculpted the path to how your mind is now. Consider how every abortion risks the creation of a traumatized abortion survivor; even if the body isn't harmed physically by an abortion, the stress still registers in the body-mind. Dr. Erik Erickson even theorized that people who struggle to implant in the womb experience the body memory as an innate sense of rejection. Can you imagine a zygote stressed out?

Are mosquitoes actually malevolent? Do they choose to be annoying? No, probably not – but it's easy to imagine that they are hateful. And in our imaginations, where do they store and cherish their hate? Not in their wings, nor in their legs, nor in their little bellies that they want to fill with your blood. It's not even in their poky little stiletto noses. It's all in their brains, inside their heads, behind their eyes. (Or so we can easily imagine.) So how big a brain do you need to find yourself accused of malevolence? Mosquito brains are tiny!

If we can imagine that mosquitoes are malevolent, why is hard to imagine that human zygotes are creative?

Pro-life education needs a whole section of imagining miniature life – mosquito brains, computer chips, robotics, and zygotes.

Math

Pro-life education needs a little math.

Suppose we chart mass and volume against age. That's not complicated. And suppose we chart "complexity," defined for the moment as the number of living cells within an organism, against age. These are pretty simple charts – of a curve that climbs rapidly at first and then flattens, starting at conception and leveling out around year 18. These curves climb very fast for a few weeks, then bend within a few months, and tip more and more as we measure years. It's noteworthy that mass and volume curves start climbing at implantation, while the complexity curve starts climbing at fertilization. The word "conception" was a synonym for "fertilization" for decades, but now many (most?) biologists use the word to refer to "implantation." Those two events are several days apart.

When we are comfortable with graphs showing mass against time, and complexity against time, we can take another step. Suppose we chart *change* in mass and *change* in complexity, against time (the "first derivative"). Those curves start high at conception (at implantation for mass, and at fertilization for complexity) and plummet, eventually flattening out at zero around age 18.

Here's the point, which is obvious if your imagination includes a little bit of mathematics: clearly, *change* reveals or suggests or defines life. And in the life of a human being, change is at its peak at conception.

The drift towards death, the steady sober encroachment of death, commences at conception. We are most alive at the explosive and creative moment of conception, and although we continue to grow for some years, we are already slowing down *on day one*.

This is not religion; it's measurable.

Physics

Back to body-minds. Yes, a zygote is a mind. No, your mind did not start with a sperm. We can clear up this confusion with statistical physics.

"Markov blankets" is a theory related to the Free Energy Principle of Karl Friston that the mind is statistically boundaried to its most complete set. In other words, we can make a reasonable guess that a mind is definitely in some locations, but not others.

The bare-bones definition of an individual mind is a "surprise-minimizing system." When I [EK] ask myself, "which subsets of markov blankets act within my surprise-minimizing system," I cannot say the sperm which donated half my DNA is clustered with the whole. This is because on its own a sperm minimizes surprise in singularity, not individuality—individual, here referring to indivisible. Now let me explain this more simply.

When I cut my hair, I don't look down and say "that's me on the floor." That hair isn't contributing to my system's perceptions in order to minimize surprise. I also wouldn't say that about my eggs if

I froze them. Same with sperm for a guy. They're divisible! For this reason I can guess that my mind was never located in a sperm.

But if you touch the living skin connected to my surprise-minimizing system, I'd say, "stop touching me." Not divisible. My zygote? Not divisible! My sophisticated ability to think in predictions is contingent upon the rudimentary perceptive ability of my zygote, my bodywide memory. Its perceptions are continuous with my system. For this reason I can guess that my mind originated in my zygote. So I was a zygote, but never a sperm.

Pro-life education should struggle to keep an educated imagination united with math and science, with STEM.

Feminist allies, eugenic opponents

A pro-life education should explain carefully that the roots of abortion are not in feminism but in eugenics. This is obviously critical today, because *most* pro-lifers today are open to the arguments made by John Tanton and his collection of population control organizations. Immigration restrictions are an integral part of global population control. If the United States is too poor or too crowded to accept and embrace millions of immigrants annually, then it follows (with very simple arithmetic) that the world is too poor or too crowded to accept and embrace tens of millions of newborn babies annually. Pro-lifers find that conclusion intolerable – and so we must teach a consistent ethic of hospitality.

Euthanasia

We note with dismay that today the pro-life movement as a whole is tightly associated with Trumpism, including vaccine denial. We could be wrong, but it is our judgment that, in rough figures, half a million people just in America died from Covid who would have lived if pro-lifers had been as serious about opposing euthanasia as we were one generation ago. The movement used to work hard to assert that we defend life from conception to a natural death, but that is no longer true. We no longer insist as a part of our commitment to life that people should make sacrifices in their comfortable lives in order to protect the elderly and weak people in our midst. Pro-lifers may or may make personal sacrifices to protect the elderly from Covid; but as a movement, pro-lifers no longer challenge others to do so. In fact, many pro-lifers use the language of their opponents, explicitly asserting the primacy of bodily integrity and personal choice over the right to life. They deny collective responsibility in the name of individualism. Euthanasia has never been as sharply defined as abortion; but pro-lifers used to prioritize life over comfort – used to, but no longer.

This poses a challenge of consistency in the movement's ethics: how can we oppose killing in cases of "incompatibility with life" and fetal anomaly, but accept reckless disregard for the infirm and the elderly? We can't claim that the sick and the disabled in the womb deserve a natural death while condemning them to death by preventable disease.

A renewed pro-life movement will return to intelligent opposition to euthanasia in our educational programs.

Embracing insights from St. John Paul II: theology of the body AND a consistent ethic of life

For Catholic pro-lifers, the careful teaching from St. John Paul II on abortion – in *Evangelium Vitae* or *The Gospel of Life* – should be required reading. But in fact, it is hard today to find anyone who follows this teaching. The encyclical asserts that abortion became a massive global slaughter following a massive shift in people's attitudes towards human sexuality. The contraceptive mentality, separating sex from procreation, can often reduce sexual activity to a delightful game. And, obviously (?), games don't create life-or-death crises, from which it follows that pregnancy must be just a minor complication, because the couples that got pregnant were just playing around. And so abortion is just a minor fix to a minor error – "obviously." The Pope explains this problem and refutes the conclusions, in his carefully developed "theology of the body." Conservative Catholics generally embrace this line of thought. But the Pope *also* carefully explains that abortion is a *life* issue, not an aberration in *sexual* matters. Abortion is best understood alongside war and capital punishment and torture and other assaults on life. Liberal Catholics are generally attracted to this "seamless garment" approach. It is rare to find people who embrace both arguments that are – both! – in *The Gospel of Life*. A healthy renewal of pro-life education will teach both.

A consistent ethic of life following the teaching of St. John Paul II will return, with solid hope and determination, to a search for common ground between pro-lifers and other activists who defend peace and justice, including:

- feminists, who assert that sexism is a grave evil that we must end;
- peace activists, who remind us that the indiscriminate slaughter of children and innocent civilians is murder, is unjustifiable;
- labor activists, who complete a balanced and beautiful icon of the Holy Family, with Mary the Mother on one side and Joseph the Worker on the other side and Jesus the innocent child with eternal dignity and worth in the center;
- environmental activists, who have their eyes fixed on future generations who deserve just treatment even though they are not yet born.

War and abortion

I [JCOK] came into the pro-life movement from the peace movement. Both of my brothers fought in Vietnam, but I was a conscientious objector. I spent most of my adult life thinking about how to protect unborn children and reconcile generations; but I never lost track of what our nuclear-armed nation was doing about world peace. And I'd like to look again at the links between (a) slaughtering unborn children *without* killing everyone else, via abortion, and (b) slaughtering unborn children *while* killing everyone else, via nuclear war.

The Second Vatican Council condemned nuclear war and abortion in similar terms: I accept that teaching as authoritative. I was with Dan Berrigan when he spoke at a Catholic Peace Fellowship meeting in Massachusetts and declared simply that "war is abortion and abortion is war." He said he had a grim hope that resisting abortion might motivate people to face the violence in our midst, and then resist war as well; what might catch people's attention in the first place with abortion was that "abortion is so personally maiming." I admire Berrigan, and I accept the wisdom of his grim insight.

In my own thinking, I make two major links – about the global impact of each of these forms of massive violence, and about nonviolence.

During the war in Vietnam, the peace movement was strong. The Cuban crisis had awakened Americans to the threat of global annihilation, and peaceniks organized against that. But the draft during the war forced all young men to pay attention. When the draft ended, the threat of nuclear annihilation was unchanged, but it was easier to ignore it. And during this time with its temptation to amnesia, the peace movement dwindled.

The Catholic Church never wavered in our opposition to nuclear war. However, when the teaching became concrete and therefore nuanced, nearly everyone in America lost track of it. The teaching from the Church, as I understand it, has several pieces that require careful attention; in a time when few Catholics or other Christians can make their way through the Commandments, all ten in a row, it's foolish to expect people to follow and understand let alone embrace a nuanced teaching. But I do, and we must.

The indiscriminate slaughter of civilians is a crime against humanity that deserves unhesitating and unequivocal condemnation. However, in our time, the possession of nuclear weapons and the threat to use them in retaliation if we are attacked with nukes – mutually assured destruction – has prevented the use of nukes for decades. This deterrence is based on a threat to do something that is completely evil: if the Russians or Chinese obliterate our civilians, we will attack and obliterate theirs. "Theirs"? "Theirs," those over there, are children of God.

The Church's response to this strategy of deterrence is clear, but with soft edges. The Church condemns the use of nukes but does not condemn possession. What in the world does that mean? We don't store them in museums; we have them so we can threaten to use them; and although some of them are packed away a little, they can be unwrapped if a "need" arises. The American government is ready and willing and able to destroy the cities of anyone who attacks us with weapons of mass destruction.

Deterrence has worked for decades. But it is based on a credible threat to kill innocent civilians including women and children. To do so would be unequivocally evil. But ...

Are we trapped in this MADness?

The Church has *not* walked away from this tangled moral question. The Church asserts firmly that the Lord has not left us stranded amidst violence. Nor does the Lord simply ask us to prepare to die well. The world has *not* been abandoned to the powers of darkness. There is a way out of the trap, and the Church supports that difficult path – leaving details of implementation to laymen with expertise but declaring unequivocally that it is possible to find a way out.

The Church notes that a way out is a global body with enough authority to disarm nuclear states. Does the Church teach that Jesus Christ supports the United Nations? Of course not! But the Church does teach that we can escape from a social evil of massive proportions, by way of something like the United Nations.

There are many obstacles to building a global authority. The League of Nations failed. The United Nations has done many good things but has had some failures and may have crippling structural flaws that may require a whole new start. But a way out of our dependence on grave evil – the threat to kill children as the basis of our defense of ourselves – does exist. And so it would be gravely evil on our part to give up on it.

One of the oddest realities of life in the 21st century is that the greatest obstacle to an effective global body that slowly builds the authority it needs to bring about nuclear disarmament may be *Christians* – conservative narrow-minded Christians who do not think that Jesus is smart enough to find his way out of trap, or perhaps that Jesus is smart, but the Church he founded is unable to discern the truth and the light and the way.

It seems to us [JCOK and EK] that the world faces several massive structures of evil that cannot be taken down without global cooperation. That includes war, and immigration – and abortion. When American pro-lifers summon the courage to face the fact that abortion is actually about 20 times worse than we [pro-lifers] have generally reckoned, then we can perhaps start thinking about how much we need to do, and we can stop tinkering with legislative efforts that are only slightly more significant than zoning regulations. Right now, we don't have the courage even to try to summon the energy we need. We doubt that Jesus can save the world. Sure, sure, something holy in heaven later on – but he can't stop nukes or global abortion. He can't; we can't. We just have to live with it – and the best we can do is keep it at a little distance.

Facing war forces us to think about how to build effective global organizations. And that makes it possible to start thinking clearly about ending abortion.

The tasks are daunting, way beyond our imagination. But (1) Jesus is Lord and the Church teaches that there is a way out; and (2) while nukes changed warfare in the 20th century, Gandhi showed that nonviolence in the 20th century has as much power as nukes.

About 40 years ago, I [JCOK] went to jail for a few days with Mike Bray for a sit-in in Montgomery County, probably at Metropolitan Family Planning in Gaithersburg. At that time, Mike was already bombing clinics, but I didn't know. As far as I knew, he supported nonviolence; he was working with the Prolife Nonviolent Action Project which usually asked for a pledge of nonviolence before a sit-in. I was deceived. So I wasn't paying careful attention to hugely important undercurrents of a friendly debate we had while we were in jail at Seven Locks. We argued about the best way to respond to Soviet aggression. This was in the mid-1980s, and the Soviet Union was still in place. I said the Poles offered the best model; he said the Afghans did. Nonviolence versus violence, in a different setting. It was clear, although not explicit, that we were actually arguing about the best way to respond to abortion in America.

In retrospect, with 20/20 hindsight, I think it's obvious that the Polish model was best. Their success destroyed the Warsaw Pact, and then the Soviet Union – in a victory that was at least as significant as defeating the Nazis in World War II, arguably far more significant. To be sure, there were other forces at work; in history and in real life, there are always other forces at work. But what the Poles did was the key. Pro-lifers should adopt the lesson, and study what they did, because the task we face is larger than what the Poles faced. We must learn from the Poles! The Afghans, on the other hand, are still at war, still mired in violence and poverty: may God have mercy on them and give them peace.

My point here is simple. Thinking about how to escape from the scourge of war and the trap of nuclear weapons helps us, if we wish to learn, to think about how to respond to abortion. Abortion is a personal decision, one child at a time; but it is also a global catastrophe, a massive structure of evil. And we have to think about how to respond to it on all levels of human experience.

EK: One cannot fully comprehend the massive structure of evil that is abortion without examining its ties to the corrupted late-stage capitalism. (I will not suggest alternative economic systems here.) The socioeconomic inequality perpetuated by its profits-over-people ethos leads to exploitation of the vulnerable for the profit and power of the privileged. This is why the poor, people of color, and immigrants are predated upon by the abortion industry.

JCOK: Socialist! Just kidding.

EK: Haha. Anyhow, if we don't break down the pillars of power that uphold and protect abortion as an industrial complex, then we stand no chance of ending its violence. All sectors must divest from Big Abortion: media, academia, government... and most importantly, the general population. If they withdraw their consent from and cooperation with the industry, it will crumble.

JCOK: And how do we convince your average Jane to do that?

EK: We empower her to survive sans violence against posterity. We use direct action to take out the intermediaries from community defense and resource distribution and give power back to the people. Meeting her material needs through pregnancy aid is a great start. Mutual aid is even better. And rescue –

> JCOK: – is life-affirming. We need pro-life nonviolence.

Direct action and abortion

My [EK] introduction to nonviolent direct action (NVDA) was through the Black Lives Matter Movement in the summer of 2020. Direct action takes collective action to instigate change without introducing a middleman. In this case, the people of color, students, and radicals of Richmond, Virginia were fed up with local police brutality, especially against racial minorities, and we decided to take our community's defense into our own hands. The direct actions agitated the cops, local policy makers, and powerful residents directly to stop the violence against Black bodies. And in some cases, we took action to stop it ourselves.

I served as a bike marshal, which is basically a bodyguard for protesters that uses their bike as a shield. (Yes, I wore all black and a mask. Yes, I was antifa. And I still consider myself anti-fascist.) I physically interposed myself between the protesters and the police. We removed police as the middlemen, instead inserting ourselves between the oppressed and their oppressors. I did it because I loved the Black protesters and knew I could use my privilege and power as a white body to protect them. I stood, literally, in solidarity.

So when I first heard about rescue as nonviolent direct action against abortion, it resonated with my experience as a bike marshal. Rescue asks us to put our bodies between the oppressed preborn people and the abortionist oppressors, because the police won't stop the violence. But I can take action to stop it myself, because I love the preborn and can use my privilege and power as a born body to protect them. When the cops don't keep us safe, we keep us safe, and the babies are us. *We* rescue us.

A better world is possible, and it starts with us prefiguring it by acting like it's already here. In rescue, we stay with the preborn like they are already recognized as people who deserve our solidarity. When we face consequences in court, we talk about the babies as equal people who deserve our defense. We do all of this in the discipline of radical hope that one day preborn legal personhood will be a reality. (And perhaps with the hypocritical outrage coming from the left over the unborn Palestinians slaughtered by missiles, we are closer than ever.)

Study NVDA! Nonviolent conflict is a social science. I highly recommend looking into Otpor in Serbia and their struggle for democracy. Srdja Popović, spokesperson of the student movement said, "We were a group of fans of life, and we won because we loved life." Also explore the roots of the Chipko "treehugger" movement, and the sacrifice of 363 protesters in 1730 that inspired it. These protesters were willing to die to save the trees for their progeny; how much more should we be willing to sacrifice our time, relationships, and way of life to save the lives of our babies?

The discipline of nonviolence

The pro-life movement must teach people to understand nonviolence, whether or not they are engaged in a campaign of nonviolent action right now. The incredible success of nonviolence in the Philippine Revolution offers an insight and a model: the revolution ousted a dictator in two weeks because they knew what they were doing – because millions of Filipinos had two decades of teaching and training in nonviolence before the uprising. We too need extensive and widespread training; we need millions of people who understand nonviolence.

I [JCOK] note with interest that the King Memorial in DC is a powerful and moving exhibit, but the powerful words on the walls there do not include any mention of King's motivation, the heart of his life – that is, Jesus – nor any mention of his life's work – that is, nonviolence. Pro-lifers studying King's work need to go back to King's own words, not just excerpts presented by ignorant or anti-Christian admirers.

So pro-life education in our time must be comprehensive, extensive. And yet, at the same time, we are always aiming for a simple insight. We recall the KISS principle: "keep it simple, stupid." Amidst our study, we aim for an "ah-ha" moment: life begins at the beginning, not the middle, and all humans are people, and we shouldn't kill each other.

To rebuild: third, nonviolent action to change hearts

Pro-life education has to cover more material than was necessary 50 years ago. We aim for a moment when a lightbulb turns on with a click: life begins at the beginning, duh. But it's hard to get there, for several reasons, including one easily discernible reason and one deeper and more challenging reason.

The easy one is that pro-lifers almost always ignore the strongest pro-abortion "argument," the strongest idea that keeps people in the pro-abortion camp. It's not a logical argument; it's ad hominem: "Don't be a goddam ass like the anti-choice fanatics over there." For sure, snobbery shouldn't keep people on the side of massive bloody violence – but for sure, it does. That's reality, and we cannot afford to ignore that reality! But we do ignore it! Often, we think it's virtuous to be content when we are perceived as repulsive.

EK: So you're saying, we should be hot.

JCOK: That's not exactly where I was going with that, and I'd expect trouble if I said that, but I'm not saying otherwise.

EK: The pro-life movement has a serious image problem. When pro-choicers picture a pro-lifer, the person they imagine lacks sex appeal. While superficial, it's a real problem when we're also accused of being anti-sex. We visually confirm that bias.

JCOK: Are you suggesting that we sexualize the movement?

EK: No! But I am saying, hot sells, and that's a huge advantage the pro-choice movement has over us. They're marketing an aesthetic. People flock to it because it looks cool. As my friend Terrisa Bukovinac says, "If it's not hot, no one cares." We don't have an appealing aesthetic, and we need to get one.

JCOK: So all I was saying is don't be repulsive. You're saying not only that, but also, look cool.

EK: Yes. It's a visual challenge to stereotypes. I think we won't overcome the obstacle of snobbery unless we pay attention to how pro-choicers look, or how they want to look. Otherwise it's too easy to "other" us.

Vanity is not a good thing, but deliberately choosing to be unapproachable weakens our ability to convince people to choose life. And weakening a pro-life witness can lead promptly to abortion. When we are repulsive, deliberately or carelessly, that's flatly pro-abortion. An example to clarify: when a sidewalk counselor wears a MAGA cap, a large portion of the country sees a loud announcement that this stranger who wants to butt into private lives in a time of pain and suffering is a violent dishonest misogynist racist. The cap enrages millions of people. In the name of God, why would a counselor carelessly erect that kind of obstacle to engagement? In the USA today, there are tens of millions of people who do not know, and do not want to know, any Trump supporters. So, does the counselor want to save a child's life *or* exchange bitter slogans across a deep political divide: *take your pick*.

The second "argument" is much deeper. It's about loyalty. It's rarely made explicit, but if you pay attention, you can see it in our opponents' eyes, smoldering with resentment or blazing with anger: "I will not let you call my beloved mother/sister/friend/whoever a murderer!" Perhaps we don't recall insulting this friend, and are appalled to learn that our words were taken that way. But when we assert that life begins at the beginning, that may seem to imply logically that etc, etc. We may not notice it when an intellectual argument turns into a loyalty test packed with violent emotion. We may not see it; and even if we do see it, we may not be able to get the issue out in the open. What pro-lifers must understand and grip tightly is that loyalty is a good and glorious thing, an extraordinarily significant part of the lives of all good people, and it's profoundly evil to brush it aside carelessly! So we scramble in the dark, brushing against a well-hidden shame, bumping into barriers erected to avoid bringing someone else's secrets into the open, threatening to force a choice between truth and loyalty.

For everyone (including Christians): this is not an intellectual struggle; this is an non-rational battle. We are up against nervous systems that have been dysregulated by trauma. Our message is perceived as a threat, triggering trauma responses. We cannot reason with trauma. Everyone has to integrate their trauma in their own time, and all we can do is hold space for that. It is only after they have made peace with their pasts that we can reach them on a deeper level. For Christians (specifically): this is a spiritual battle. It is not enough to aim for a change of *mind*; that's ludicrously insufficient. In the dark, we plead for the Lord's guidance, because we aim blindly for a change of *heart*. It is not enough to *convince*; we must aim to *convert*.

It is perplexing when pro-lifers say year after year, "I can't understand how anyone can be pro-abortion!" – and then, having admitted total ignorance, launch into a speech. Wouldn't it be better to listen and understand, and *then* argue?

Pro-life nonviolent action is what we need in such a spiritual battle. Nonviolence is not just an acknowledgment that we are fighting powers and principalities, pressing against demonic forces. We're pressing against the darkest parts of the human condition. It's not an *acknowledgment*; it's *pushing back*. The power that we bring to the struggle is the power of self-sacrificial love and forgiveness. In our time, we need new words and new approaches to understand ancient truths: the Church says that the new name for *peace* is *progressio* (English: *development*), and the new name for *love* is *solidarity*. Similarly, I [JCOK] would urge, the new name for *repentance* is *nonviolence*. We don't need these new words to handle every personal problem, but we do need them to respond to the social issues of our time like war and racism and abortion. Nonviolence! We need the word, and the concept, and the action.

Since 1891, when Pope Leo XIII wrote "Rerum Novarum," we have been challenged to see and understand and respond to "res novae" or "new things." The *Baltimore Catechism*, completed in 1885, before Pope Leo's encyclical about new things, does not explain how to respond to the "res novae" of our time. In ages past, Christians could and did live Christian lives thinking about *personal* and *spiritual* issues; that worked. But for the past 132+ years, the Church has asked us to think and pray and act in response to another dimension of human life – urgent *social* issues, the "res novae" of this time in history.

The Church asks us to think in ways that the *Baltimore Catechism* doesn't explain. Let me recall an example. When my [JCOK] sister Kathie confronted her own abortion, she admitted her own personal responsibility and went to confession – that's a *personal* response and then a *spiritual* response. But also, in addition, she wanted to understand how it could happen that it ever made sense to her to have an abortion. What was going on in the world so that all of her devout Catholic friends, and she herself, could think that abortion was a solution to anything? She was not in any way denying or minimizing her own personal responsibility, but she wanted to understand what had happened in society – the "res novae" of the 1960s. She wanted to understand the *social* realities, and then find a spiritual response to new *social evils*. That determination led to her life-long study of eugenics, the incredibly destructive ideology that helped to shape the minds and hearts of Stalin and Hitler and Mao and Sanger. And in time, that led her into a social response to a social evil, beyond argumentation: she joined a campaign of nonviolent action.

A key piece of the Church's teaching about social evils in our time is St. John Paul II's apostolic exhortation "On Reconciliation and Penance." He defines "social sin" carefully, and he explains the interface between social sin and personal sin. Often, he explains, we participate in massive social evils by personal sins of omission, by carelessness or cowardice.

EK: The secular equivalent of social sin is being complicit, and thereby culpable, in perpetuating the violence of oppressive systems, usually through cooperation.

> JCOK: *Let's be patient with Catholics as they adapt to the terminology of secular social justice circles.*

Repentance for social evils is not identical to repentance for personal sins. The route to liberation from massive social evils is solidarity with the victims of that evil. And to be transformative, that solidarity must be expressed in self-sacrificial love, in nonviolent action.

What Gandhi showed is that love can indeed be social and political and national and global. Whatever violence can do – that is, whatever good war can accomplish – love and nonviolence can match. Gandhi's achievement is as large as George Washington's. And the Solidarity movement led by Lech Walesa and encouraged by Pope John Paul II was as liberating and transformative as World War II.

To rebuild: fourth, political action to change laws

I must repeat and re-emphasize, maybe shouting from the rooftops: changing the law comes at the end of a long process. In my understanding, the whole pro-life movement since the 1970s has been engaged in a damn fool errand, trying to change the law without bothering to change society. This has never worked in the entire recorded history of the human race. There are two ways to bring about a change that large: war or campaign of nonviolence. (In prior ages, a campaign of nonviolence was called "a time of persecution.") History does not offer a third option.

Slavery in America was ended by a war. It was impossible to end slavery before the war; it was almost inevitable that we would end slavery after the war. The *war* changed American society; the *law* followed after. After!

One day, at some time in the future, a new generation will change the law concerning protection for the unborn. But it is ludicrous to think we will do so now. To get from here to there, we need a massive social change brought about by a massive campaign of nonviolence. Then we can talk about changing the law.

The task is global. This global perspective is, of course, shared by the Church, which teaches that we are called to love all our brothers and sisters – regardless of age and stage of development – *around the world*. But it is also plain common sense. The people who started the pro-life movement two generations ago grew up in time when about two percent of the people in the United States went abroad each year. It made sense then to expect that ending abortion within America would make a real difference. But today, about 40 percent of Americans go abroad annually. So now, ending abortion in America but not in Mexico or Sweden is not a big change; it's a little better than a zoning regulation, but not a lot better. Going abroad for an abortion is more expensive than driving to the city, but the added expense is something that most – not all, but most – Americans can afford. Ending abortion in America but not elsewhere will prevent the poor from aborting; that's not meaningless, but it is a small part of the real task we face, and it looks mean. Think global – or shut up.

The new pro-life movement must accept and embrace and pay attention to major allies – beginning with the Catholic Church but including all religious groups – most obviously Protestants and Muslims. Today, the American pro-life movement is loaded with people who pick and choose among Protestant leaders, who pick and choose among Catholic teachings, and who reject Muslims with fiery disrespect and even contempt.

I [JCOK] note that St. John Paul II spoke and wrote about a new "culture of life and civilization of love." His understanding of that culture and civilization includes defense of the unborn – *and of all God's people facing injustice and violence*. But when pro-lifers refer to his teaching, they ignore most of it – blissfully unaware of their narrow-minded censorship of his words, even in the teaching that is explicitly labeled *The Gospel of Life*. Amazing.

The Catholic Church – the ecumenical catholic church – is our key ally. So pro-life leaders who make a point of attacking Vatican II or the Pope may or may not be building the movement with one hand; I'm not sure about that. But I am sure they are slashing and smashing the movement with the other hand. The Church claims to teach with apostolic authority. If a pro-lifer rejects that authority regarding many issues (peace and justice issues in particular), that same pro-lifer cannot claim the backing of that same authority regarding abortion. That's not a small loss. To be clear: pro-lifers who quote Cardinal Burke and Archbishop Schneider and Bishop Strickland and Fr. Altman and other dissidents *claim to be following* the Church on abortion, but *in fact are rejecting* the Church's teaching on a long list of related issues. They build with one hand and tear down with the other, giving scandal and undercutting the Church's authority.

When the pro-life movement is rebuilt some time in the future, the new pro-life leaders will reach out proactively and build alliances, not reject them with some kind of purifying blowtorch. But with each passing year we are caught in the nasty mesh of Trumpism, the movement's task of building bridges gets harder and harder. We need pro-life feminists; we need to be tied tightly to the peace movement; we need immigrants; we need the habit of imagining a just future that environmentalists offer; we need to balance family and life issues and labor issues. Why in the name of God don't Catholic pro-lifers ever read St. John Paul II's *Compendium of the Social Doctrine of the Church*? You don't have to be some kind of leftie loonie to long for a broad-minded and honest consistency! What a joy it can be to meet a faithful Catholic who actually listens and tries to cooperate with the Church – the one united with the Pope, not the flimsy plastic imitation based on American nostalgia.

A movement that aims for a new "culture of life and civilization of love" is substantially more ambitious than aiming for a change in the law in one nation. That can seem daunting! But an expanded vision doesn't have to mean more work for the same faithful few. It is more work, but for far more people. Alliances strengthen all of us.

Leaning left

Speaking of allies, I [EK] have observed that the critical frameworks of many left-leaning social justice movements are compatible – if not parallel – with pro-life ideology. What I mean by that is, I see us saying very similar things, just in different contexts. This compels me to believe that liberals and leftists already have the values in place which compel them to protect all people; they just don't understand embryos and fetuses to be people as pro-lifers do. Let me share some of their slogans with you to illustrate.

In 2024, a common refrain of the pro-Palestinian movement is "Fund care, not killing." This could easily be a reference to funding pregnancy aid centers rather than abortion businesses. Another: "No pride in genocide." If you see abortion as the mass slaughter of a particular class of people, then this is applicable.

In the pro-immigration movement, they often say "no human is illegal." Prenates are human, but not recognized as people legally; could one say their current status is illegal human? From the animal rights movement comes the phrase, "I pray nobody kills me for the crime of being small." Could this be the plea of an embryo about to be aborted? A slogan of the Black Lives Matter movement is,

"Respect existence or expect resistance." Could this point to the moment a new human organism is formed?

I have also seen anti-fascists share memes that say, "Everyone has the right to life." From a radical feminist account: "Any world where people, en masse, are exterminated is not a free world." And from a mutualist anarchist: "Love is justice, a commitment to the sanctity of all human lives." You can't make this stuff up. This is from their own mouths.

Liberals are not demons who reject love and life; in fact, they embrace it. But they have subscribed to a covert eugenicist ideology about which humans are the "right kind" to be people, and that valuing the "wrong kind" of humans as equal is dehumanizing to ourselves. If we successfully help key influencers break away from their belief in a "right kind" of human, then it will only be a matter of time before our numbers expand dramatically. We don't have to evangelize conservatism to make leftwing folks anti-abortion; we can convert them to be pro-life by drawing upon their pre-existing values system! We have to signal-boost leftists already in the movement who can speak their language and teach it to us as well.

Abortion can be non-partisan. This is how we will build political power for the movement and majority support for pro-life legislation: not by growing the right, but by carving out an anti-abortion left.

The vision and internal unity of St. John Paul II

We know who has been fighting to protect unborn children for the longest: the Catholic Church. And know who will keep fighting without giving in to exhaustion or fear: the Catholic Church. But only a few pro-lifers pay attention to the Church's approach! It's spelled out in a document that's not hidden, not written in code: it's *The Gospel of Life*. And that document is a key piece of a larger body of Church teaching which is also labeled clearly: *The Compendium of the Social Doctrine of the Church*.

The pro-life movement doesn't want, doesn't need, and can't have a movement that is exclusively Catholic. But we do want, do need, and can have a movement that draws on the ancient wisdom of that church, guided by the spirit of Jesus Christ. Catholic or not, we can draw on the Catholic Church. It's worthwhile – in fact, urgent – to explore this *Compendium*, and in particular, to see how the right to life fits within it.

The *Compendium* is not a laundry list of issues. It's a carefully constructed explanation of the way social justice fits into evangelization, and a careful explanation of the development of the Social Gospel since 1891. Still, the *Compendium* does pay attention to some specific issues – mostly the same ones that were singled out by the Second Vatican Council. (*Gaudium et Spes*, 40 years before the *Compendium*, stated, "Of the many subjects arousing universal concern today, it may be helpful to concentrate on these: marriage and the family, human progress, life in its economic, social and political dimensions, the bonds between the family of nations, and peace.") It may be interesting and useful to pull out from the *Compendium* a dozen specific issues for discussion, so that honest and thoughtful pro-lifers can see how abortion fits into the social doctrine of the Church.

So, the 12 issues in the *Compendium*:

1. abortion (see especially chapter 3)
2. universal healthcare: a right (see especially chapters 4 and 9)
3. family life (see chapter 5)
4. labor (see chapter 6)
5. immigration (see especially chapter 6)
6. inequality: wealth exists to be shared (see chapter 7)
7. racism: democracy and defense of minorities (see chapter 8)
8. one world government (see chapter 9)
9. environment (see chapter 10)
10. nuclear disarmament (see chapter 11)
11. doctrine and *Rerum Novarum* [New Things] (see chapter 12)
12. civilization of love (see conclusion)

1. Abortion

The right to life does not have its own chapter in the *Compendium*, but it is addressed throughout the document, especially in chapter 3 which focuses on human rights. It is clearest in paragraph 155, which has a list of rights taken from John Paul II's encyclical *Centesimus Annus*. A key idea in the pro-life movement is affirmed here: "The first right presented in this list is the right to life, from conception to its natural end, which is the condition for the exercise of all other rights and, in particular, implies the illicitness of every form of procured abortion and of euthanasia."

How important is it to understand the right to life within a larger context, like the Church's social doctrine or some such framework of justice? The *Compendium* (in paragraph 156), is clear: "Those, therefore, who claim their own rights, yet altogether forget or neglect to carry out their respective duties, are people who build with one hand and destroy with the other."

2. Universal healthcare

It does seem intuitively obvious that the right to life includes the right to healthcare, since healthcare can almost be defined as a collection of techniques for protecting life. But the sociological and political fact remains: many pro-lifers are vehemently opposed to universal healthcare, or Obamacare, or any such "Socialist" idea.

This hesitation about linking the right to life and the right to healthcare is incomprehensible. It is easy to separate "socialism" from universal healthcare, unless you allow yourself to be scared off by the phrase "socialized medicine." Social control of the means of production is one thing, and it is indeed a prominent target for conservatives, and it's condemned by the Catholic Church. On the other hand, the Church's social doctrine begins with a clear and forceful denunciation of Socialism tied to a clear and forceful defense of social action – strikes in particular – on behalf of workers. The Church denounces Socialism and praises action for social justice in 1891, and consistently ever since. It's just plain ignorant to confuse the two! The Church does not claim any special expertise in labor relations, but does claim expertise in human dignity; if the dignity of workers requires strikes, the Church supports strikes. Social control of production is one thing; social services and social justice are another. This is not complicated.

Pro-lifers are justifiably proud of pregnancy aid programs, including sidewalk counseling. But notice what pro-lifers offer in these settings. We offer, first and foremost, hope: it is possible to protect the lives of helpless children and also lead a full and successful life yourself. This is possible! Hope! But to back up this proffer of hope, pro-lifers also collect resources to ensure that women facing an unwanted pregnancy can find ways to meet a list of needs. But honesty requires that we see and admit how often pro-lifers refer women to institutions and programs that were built and funded and staffed and supported by broad coalitions loaded up with liberals and Democrats and pro-choicers! Medical help: pro-lifers and pro-choicers together offer it. Legal help: same. Education: same. Housing: same. Emergency funds: same. If pro-lifers depended exclusively on volunteer programs, funded and staffed exclusively by pro-lifers, our offers of help would shrink dramatically.

Universal healthcare coverage is a fundamental element of abortion prevention and protection of life.

But also, on the other hand: "universal" healthcare excluding the unborn isn't universal.

3. Family

Family issues get an entire chapter in the *Compendium* – "Chapter Five: The Family, the Vital Cell of Society." Linking family issues to the right to life is tricky. It is undeniable that the "contraceptive mentality" – separating sexual activity from babies – looms large in the background of abortion. But among the most important aspects of family life and family rights is the drive to protect family decisions against intrusion by government or other social entities. The decisions people make about sexual expression are certainly grist for the mill of moral philosophy – but are not obviously subject to legislation. If it is true that natural law, not just Christian morality, asserts that a marriage is between one man and one woman, then a large portion of the moral exemplars of our heritage were engaged in grave evil – not just David the murderous adulterer, but also a list of polygamists including Abraham and Isaac and Jacob and Solomon. And don't overlook 1.5 billion Muslims throughout the modern world. We don't want public school teachers explaining the mechanics of human sexuality to toddlers, and we assert the authority of parents in this matter. Exactly how, then, do we claim the right to regulate sexual behavior of consenting adults who do not share our ideas of morality? And, most important for pro-lifers: do we want to link issues that depend on a religious framework to abortion? Aren't we struggling valiantly to avoid that confusion? Abortion is a matter of life or death, not sexual morality!

Still: babies generally come from sexual activity, and it's silly and even dishonest to overlook this obvious fact. There's some deep and fascinating mystery here, worth exploring!

EK: Another issue that conservative pro-lifers love to link to abortion is "gender ideology." I implore pro-lifers not to bring up these two topics in the same breath! Gender-affirmation for consenting adults is a matter of sexual morality. The implications of associating it with abortion reinforce confusion and foster suspicion among pro-choicers. Ultimately, lumping rejection of transgenderism with opposition to abortion alienates LGBT+ folks and their allies from our cause, which is a real shame considering that they are primed to become fierce fighters for prenatal justice.

JCOK: So, for many of the same reasons I discussed above, let's stick to comparing like with like. Don't compare controversies of self-determination to interpersonal violations of human rights.

EK: It's not just unhelpful; when it comes to building trust between ourselves and our opposition, it's shooting ourselves in the foot. Leave gender ideology out of conversations about abortion (unless you want to discuss how the abortion industry preys upon pregnant gender-nonconforming individuals and intersex babies; then definitely incorporate those talking points!)

4. Labor

A balanced picture of human life and more specifically of family life includes a clear understanding of work, and a vigorous defense of workers' rights. An icon of the Holy Family includes (1) Jesus at the center as the guarantor of the overwhelming dignity of the individual, flanked by (2) Mary the Mother of her own small family and also the whole human family with zero exceptions, and (3) Joseph the Worker. The teaching of the Church is balanced; social justice beginning with the encyclical on labor is balanced with pro-life teaching that recalls Mary.

A pro-life movement that ignores workers' rights is unbalanced. A labor movement that ignores family life has been dehumanized.

EK: I would also assert that being pro-life is solidarity with the working class. While doing pro-life activism openly on the street, many working class folks have approached me to thank me for my efforts. From both research surveys and my personal experience, I surmise that the working class generally leans pro-life, despite being the demographic most vulnerable to abortion. They are the prime target of the capitalist abortion industry. When someone both believes abortion is murder and, insidiously, feels they have no other choice, we call this a "survival abortion." Solidarity with the working class prevents such abortions.

JCOK: When I was in jail in Connecticut in 1978, most of the men there were working class. To my surprise, they all agreed that abortion was killing a child – all, with zero exceptions. That's not to say they wouldn't do it, and rob someone while they were at it. But they didn't pretend it was okay. It was startling to find myself in agreement with them, and extraordinarily refreshing. So my experience supports your assertion.

5. Immigration

The *Compendium* does not have a carefully focused teaching about immigration; the teaching shows up in various chapters, including "Chapter Ten: Safeguarding the Environment." But it is relevant and noteworthy that the apostolic exhortation *Familiaris*

Consortio includes a list of rights of the family, and the right to migrate is among them.

The next generation of the world comes from births, of course; but the next generation of the United States or any nation comes from births and immigration. Any eugenic plan to shape the next generation will focus on births and immigration. Hungary, for example, wants Hungary to remain Hungarian; and so the current government was elected on a platform with two explicit complementary pieces – encouraging Hungarian births and excluding Muslim immigrants. This is not a pro-life plan; this is racist eugenics.

When the American eugenics movement was at its peak in the 1920s, it launched several initiatives:

- preventing births among dysgenic people by compulsory sterilization of the "feeble-minded";
- maintaining the vitality and genetic purity of desirable families by prohibiting "miscegenation," marriage between whites and people of various colors;
- sharply limiting immigration from nations ("races") of colored people.

The first and second of these initiatives have ended in shame and disgrace, but the third initiative is still prominent and powerful in American life.

It is impossible to offer a rational justification for limiting immigration into the relatively depopulated continent of North America without simultaneously – albeit accidentally – promoting global population control. If America is too crowded or too poor to welcome and embrace a robust influx of immigrants, then the world is far too crowded to welcome and embrace a robust influx of babies. Further, it is impossible to explain to a reluctant pregnant woman why she should welcome this child, despite the lifelong challenges the birth will bring, while simultaneously refusing to welcome healthy immigrants who will pose some challenges for a few years and then offer great benefits for decades.

We need a consistent ethic of hospitality – pro-life and pro-immigrant.

6. Inequality

Wealth exists to be shared. Decades ago, a great pro-life leader, Mike Schwartz, pointed out that poverty and overpopulation are actually the same thing, regarded from slightly different angles. Both words refer to an imbalance of people and goods. But when we talk about "poverty," people of good will feel some challenge to help out, while the word "overpopulation" seems to suggest that the problem is "their" fault. Unequal distribution of wealth in America and throughout the world poses challenges, and for some people population control and immigration restrictions are among the tools available to confront the problem. The Church rejects those "solutions," and urges a commitment to solidarity – with those in need, with facing an unplanned pregnancy, throughout the nation and throughout the world.

7. Racism

Who exactly belongs in the category of the chosen and protected "we," and who is the dreaded and rejected "them"? Both abortion and racism are based on a blind spot: some people aren't quite right, aren't fully human – because they are Black, or because they are young. The judgment of "otherness" is based on perceptions that are experienced as "obvious" and beyond question. And the people making the judgment can be completely delightful and loving and intelligent except with regard to their semi-humans. But obviously, justice is impossible unless we can locate and face and fix our prejudices! Escape from these prejudices often seems just about impossible right up until the moment of an epiphany.

EK: I'd say the pro-life movement also still has some prejudices to face. We decry eugenics, and so often bring up how Black preborn people are disproportionately aborted. We claim that we are on the right side of racial justice, that we care about all Black lives; yet somehow we've managed to make the Black community distrust us!

JCOK: How might we fix that?

EK: First, we should ask Black pro-lifers what they believe needs to be done, and we ought to listen closely. Too often we've silenced Black leaders, tokenized them, and talked over them; we must uplift them and magnify their voices. And then, we follow their lead by tailoring our approaches to harmonize with Black culture and our messages to meet the unique concerns of Black people today.

8. One world government

The Church asserts the principle of subsidiarity – that the smallest social unit that can address a problem effectively is the right one for that problem. But there are some problems that can't be faced effectively by any social unit smaller than the whole world. Those problems include modern warfare, plague, famine, poverty, migration – and, we see more and more clearly, abortion. Abortion is now a global catastrophe, and – given the rapidly expanding availability and ease of global travel – ending it within a nation is almost meaningless.

EK: That sounds intimidating and a little fatalistic.

JCOK: I understand how intimidating it can be to face a demand to think globally.

EK: *Can't we do what we can, locally? Doesn't that still matter?*

JCOK: *Of course! I think this will become clear when we start digging into rescue.*

I [JCOK] I admit freely that the way I start to face the immensity of the task ahead is not available to everyone. Still, let me just point briefly at what I do in my head and heart, which may be available to others after some adjustments.

First, of course, I'm a Christian, and I believe that Jesus Christ is the Lord of the universe, and the world is an important detail in his responsibilities. I am not the savior of the world, but I believe that I know who is, and I work for him. I don't have to figure out how to fix everything; I am responsible for understanding his work more and more each day, trying to respond to the promptings of his Spirit, finding a way to contribute.

Second – related but not identical – I am Catholic, and my church is committed to the development (in Latin, *progressio*) of everyone everywhere in every way – the development of every facet of human life including physical and mental and emotional and spiritual and economic and political. I don't have to *understand* all that; I *support* that labor in all its detailed glory (see the *Compendium of the Social Doctrine of the Church*), and try to find my place within it.

Third, much less important but still significant: I'm a Harvard graduate, so I have friends and classmates (and opponents) all around the world doing thousands of globally relevant things. I listen and laugh and love and support or oppose – but my acquaintances share a global perspective.

Government at every level is subject to abuse and incompetence and corruption. Nonetheless, the quaint villages of the past are, well, of the past. A global problem requires a global solution, even if we have yet to build the structures we need.

Today, most nations refuse to protect the unborn by law. And the United Nations shows itself to tend pro-abortion whenever the question arises. This is a challenge, but not a reason to despair and walk away.

What is the largest global organization today? It's not the UN, nor the World Bank, nor the International Court of Justice, nor the USA, nor the Gates Foundation. Without any serious competition, it's the Catholic Church. That doesn't mean that the world is just about to be perfect, but it does mean that people who despair of building effective and just and peaceful global structures are simply not paying attention to reality. We have a long way to go, but we have started.

Again: pro-lifers need the UN or something like it, and the UN or its successor needs pro-lifers.

9. Environment

Who cares deeply about future generations, and tries to protect the unborn? Pro-lifers, of course, are focused on protecting the lives of the unborn. But environmentalists are also focused on future generations, working to protect their property rights. The world in which we live belongs to them as well as to us; we must share it with them. Seizing irreplaceable goods from the world for the use of one or two generations is theft, pure and simple.

Pro-lifers and environmentalists protect the lives and the property of our descendants. It's crazy that we are not trying to cooperate as often as possible.

EK: You know who else cares deeply about future generations?

JCOK: I know you are about to explain something I haven't thought about. Who?

EK: The trauma-informed movement! They're trying to break intergenerational cycles of trauma so as to not pass any on. They're also waking up to in-utero trauma, and the consequent importance of reducing stressors upon parents and their bodies.

JCOK: Including stressors from the global environment.

EK: Nice connection. I want pro-lifers to make the trauma-informed movement more aware of abortion survivors, because so many report complex post-traumatic stress symptoms. This is further proven by the survivors of selective-reduction abortion, in which a fetus is killed while their sibling is spared. Can you imagine spending six months with the remains of your sibling next to you?

JCOK: Nope. Or maybe a little, but not accurately.

EK: Research is proving that the survivor will experience worse health outcomes throughout life due to the stress of the abortion. Ultrasounds during these procedures have also shown the survivors flailing and wriggling; a sign of distress. It's obvious that the hostile environment abortion introduced into the womb impacted them for life. I think that's another point of cooperation.

JCOK: Interesting, as I expect from you. But let me emphasize my point from a Christian perspective: "Thou shalt not kill" the next generation and "Thou shalt not steal" from the next generation are related commandments.

10. Nuclear disarmament

Abortion kills children without killing everyone else. Nuclear war kills children while killing everyone else. Killing children is an abomination, either way.

The Church asserts firmly that humanity is not caught permanently and hopelessly in the trap of mutually assured destruction. For decades, the world has in fact prevented nuclear war by ensuring all relevant parties that there will not be any victors in a nuclear war: everyone will be devastated – so no rational person will start it. But that scheme of deterrence depends on the tested and credible will to carry out retaliation if attacked. And that retaliation means destroying cities-full of children, among other horrors. So that's inexcusable. Further, the deterrence scheme has worked for decades, but its history does not prove that it's stable. We need a way out. And the way out that the Church promotes and that sane leaders throughout the world have been working to build since 1948 is a global authority that has enough authority to disarm nuclear states. Obviously, we are not there yet – but there is a way out of despair.

Curiously, among the major obstacles to strengthening the United Nations are conservative Americans, including most leaders of the pro-life movement.

It is possible that during the major shifts in the pro-life plans after the *Dobbs* decision, pro-lifers may notice that abortion is now a global phenomenon that cannot be solved by individual nations. It is possible that this realization, once grasped firmly, will change the way pro-lifers think about an effective global authority.

Post-*Dobbs* reality may finally shove pro-lifers into listening to the wise (and, for some, authoritative) teaching of the Catholic Church (*Compendium*, 441). "Concern for an ordered and peaceful coexistence within the human family prompts the Magisterium to insist on the need to establish some universal public authority acknowledged as such by all and endowed with effective power to safeguard, on the behalf of all, security, regard for justice, and respect for rights."

11. [for Catholics] Doctrine

Oftentimes, it seems that the Church is threatened by a schism, setting pro-lifers against advocates of social justice. But the *Compendium* situates the right to life firmly embedded within social justice teaching.

When he asked for a new document collecting and disseminating the Church's rich teaching about social justice, St. John Paul II said that there was a gaping hole in the catechesis that most Catholics received – cradle Catholics as well as new converts. So, just exactly how important is this vast body of new teaching that has grown up since the publication of *Rerum Novarum* in 1891? It's "indispensable." Paragraph 524: "The Church's social teaching is the indispensable reference point that determines the nature, modality, articulation and development of pastoral activity in the social field. It is the expression of the ministry of social evangelization, aimed at enlightening, stimulating and supporting the integral promotion of the human person through the practice of Christian liberation in its earthly and transcendent dimension."

EK: For everyone, this is basically a Catholic way of saying "our liberation is bound together" and "no one is free until all of us are free." All justices are dependent upon each other; there is no racial justice without environmental justice; there is no economic justice without disability justice; there is no social justice without prenatal justice. As long as we see some humans as disposable, all human life will be treated as disposable.

JCOK: There is no liberation without the unborn.

Of course I [JCOK] want everyone who cares about peace and justice to be aware of the teaching from an ally, the Catholic Church. But my point, this 11th point I want to make about the *Compendium*, is relevant to faithful Catholics and not necessarily to anyone else:

the *Compendium* collects and explains "doctrine." The Catholic Church asserts that the Apostles and their successors were given the authority to explain the meaning of Scripture – to teach, for example, that the commandment not to steal includes something that Catholics a century ago might not have thought about very much: it includes a commandment to protect the treasures of the earth that our descendants will inherit. For people who accept the authority of claimed by the Catholic Church, the authority to teach about faith and morals, this little word "doctrine" packs a wallop.

12. Civilization of love

Pro-lifers often invoke the words of St. John Paul II about a "culture of life and a civilization of love" to undergird their work. That's great, perhaps; it's encouraging. But pro-life work is a piece, not the whole, of this new culture and civilization. The teaching from the Pope is clear and forceful – and visible in the *Compendium*. The civilization to which he refers is explicitly pro-life *and pro-justice*. The *Compendium*, with all 12 chapters, offers his vision. To pull out a single piece of that vision and then to ignore the rest and even oppose substantial parts, and then to pretend that you and the Pope are talking about the same vision: that's either deplorably ignorant or flatly dishonest.

For a serious and educated and honest Catholic, the pro-life movement belongs in a broader context – not only within the consistent ethic of life that so many pro-lifers deplore, but more, much more. The pro-life movement belongs within an entire social justice framework.

EK: For everyone, this underscores the vital necessity of having visibility as individuals in other social justice movements. We cannot ignore other issues. We must show up, not just in word, but also in action in order to prove that we care for life and justice across the board.

> JCOK: Right. This is how we build coalitions, allies, and – perhaps more importantly – friendships. This is how others can see that we aren't just some more bigots over there in lala-land; we are in fact approachable like other human beings.

+++++++

The social doctrine of the Church, in sum

Building the "civilization of love" ... The immediate purpose of the Church's social doctrine is to propose the principles and values that can sustain a society worthy of the human person. Among these principles, solidarity includes all the others.

Part Two: Rebuilding Pro-life Nonviolence

Re-building the pro-life movement requires a new and determined focus on the great task of nonviolence. But pro-life activists have abused the term and lost track of its meaning – its history, its discipline, its power. We need to study to understand and unpack and deploy this great thing. We need to re-build pro-life nonviolence, from the ground up and the heavens down.

Jesus asks that we be perfect, and that we love our enemies, that we love other as God loves us. Gandhi showed that this kind of love can have meaning not only in individual relationships but also in all social relations.

Nonviolence, explained

> *"First they ignore you, then they laugh at you, then they fight you, then you win."*
>
> *"Jesus was the most active resister known perhaps to history. This was non-violence par excellence."*
>
> – Mahatma Gandhi

Nonviolence is not just good manners or acceptable public behavior. It's a deliberate effort to change a society or the world by a dynamic that is demonstrably as powerful as – or more powerful than – nuclear weapons. But this dynamic has its own assumptions and disciplines.

In the 1970s, many activists launched pro-life nonviolent action – in every state plus DC. In the 1980s, this came to be called the "rescue movement." Over time, the rescue movement drifted or shifted away from principled nonviolence, and became a detail of pregnancy aid and sidewalk counseling– an offer of help made at the door of an abortion clinic. That's not a bad thing, but it is very far from a campaign of nonviolence!

To begin, what does the word "nonviolence" even mean? What is this nonviolence? The word has been degraded and needs some fresh explanation. In common parlance, the word is used to mean several very different things:

- not violent
- polite and mannerly (respectability)
- harnessing the press by risking jail
- a strategy for ending social evils, a discipline taught and used by Gandhi.

Some drug offenses are called nonviolent offenses. Selling fentanyl, for example, is effectively murderous given a little time, but it's not flatly baldly murder. Buying it, stealing it, carrying it, sharing it with friends – these offenses may lead to death, but they don't necessarily involve carrying or using a gun. So when there's discussion of how much jail time to impose for drug-related crimes, some offenses are called "nonviolent." No gun = nonviolence #1.

The annual March for Life is sometimes described as nonviolent. That is, there won't be fistfights, and even hollering at pro-choice counter demonstrators is discouraged. Good manners and "peaceful" protests. Respectability politics = nonviolence #2.

Martin Luther King was committed to Gandhian nonviolence, but his followers have often confused two very different things and called both of them nonviolence. King's followers often precipitated confrontations in which they got themselves arrested and jailed – and by their sacrifice, they got sympathetic press, and they successfully publicized their calls for justice. What they did was good; we don't dispute that. But it wasn't necessarily an appeal to the heart of opponents, or not just that alone; it was also an effort to increase their visibility. Harnessing the power of the press via arrests = nonviolence #3.

Mohandas Gandhi developed a complex idea and led campaigns based on it – an idea that he found in the words of Jesus in his Sermon on the Mount. The idea is that love can be and should be a political force, that we can and should transform societies by loving our enemies, that love is effectively and demonstrably stronger than death here on earth as well as in heaven, that a cycle of violence can be broken by absorbing violence and forgiving, that forgiveness unleashes colossal power, that we should stand with the oppressed against oppression but do so without rancor, that our opponents have a conscience that we can reach and touch if we are willing to suffer patiently. Gandhi struggled to find a word or phrase to describe what he was teaching – "passive resistance" or "ahimsa" or "satyagraha" or plain old "love." He had a clear and articulate idea, but he wanted a single word to refer to it efficiently. The word he chose – the word we use today – is "nonviolence." (#4)

It's necessary to mention a fraud that some pro-lifers promote. Some pro-lifers now say that violence means a hurtful act that *violates the law*. By this understanding, when cops arrest a man who is beating a child, they subdue him with force, maybe smashing bones or even killing him. But since they act in the name of the law, their actions are not legal *violations*, and so they are "nonviolent." Further, this fraud asserts that defending others with force is not just moral but also legal, via the necessity defense. And so, they argue, shooting an abortionist is "nonviolent." We reject their ideas and actions completely, without any reservation; but we also reject their *language*. They are destroying our ability to communicate clearly. This is not an honest use of the word; it is simply fraudulent. And as the threat of "pro-life" violence looms larger and larger, it matters that people be aware of this fraud, and reject it firmly. To understand what people are saying when they use this relatively new word carved out by Gandhi and King, we have to be aware of this fifth use, this gross abuse. Nonviolence #5 = not violating a law, after limiting the meaning of "law" by adopting a natural law theory and adding to it a defense of lynching. #5 is a pompous murderous fraud. It would be a bad joke, except that I expect some more people will act on it, emulating Paul Hill and Jim Kopp and calling it "nonviolent."

So the word is tangled, and when pro-lifers use the word, we need to explain what we mean by it. When we (JCOK and EK) use the word, we are referring to the teaching and practice of Gandhi and King and Pope John Paul II and Lech Walesa and Corazon Aquino.

When Operation Rescue got started in New York, Cardinal John O'Connor supported the initiative – after he asked for and received a commitment, repeated over and over, that the actions would be nonviolent. What he meant was clear: he was referring to Gandhian nonviolence, satyagraha, the Sermon on the Mount. But some of the pro-lifers who made that commitment later backed away from it via linguistic garbage and fraud. In their view of things, they stepped up and away from nonviolence, returning to Biblical principles. In one quick "improvement" they shifted from nonviolence as in the

Sermon on the Mount to genocide as in the life of Saul. So pro-lifers struggling to return to Gandhi's term (and discipline) face a struggle!

Besides the word, there's other confusion

In American experience, not just the word but the whole idea is tangled. Martin Luther King's memorial in DC is wonderful and inspiring, but there are a couple of omissions that are bizarre and twisted. As mentioned above, the memorial has a lot of rich text and great speeches – but the name "Jesus" does not appear there, nor the word "nonviolence." So the memorial does not reflect reality; it's about a mythical black guy, 20 feet tall, only slightly more attached to reality than comic book cosmic avengers. Many of King's followers know nothing about his heart or his drive – or, knowing, opt to censor all that embarrassing nonsense. Rev. Martin Luther King, Jr, the real man, was a minister of the Gospel, a devoted disciple of Jesus Christ; it's impossible to talk about his drive, his heart, his life, without mentioning the core of his being. You are ignorant or lying about him in ways that would appall him if you skip over his love for God. And his life work was not only about racial justice. That mattered, of course; but lots of people did that, and he was different! He was successful in the struggle because he changed the shape of the struggle: he chose to strive for racial justice through *nonviolence*. The real man loved the Lord, and followed the teaching found in the Sermon on the Mount: that's who he was in reality, not just some black Batman.

Rev. Jesse Jackson used to promote himself as a successor to King's mantle, but that claim has huge problems. Jackson did many good things, and he fought hard for racial justice; but he was not honest and principled like his mentor. He started well; but then, it seems, he slipped away. For one thing, Jackson said, at a meeting of the National Youth Pro-Life Coalition in 1977, that the logic of abortion is the same as the logic of slavery. He said he would have been killed by abortion if he had been conceived after *Roe v. Wade*. He said his pro-life grandmother saved him and raised him. And so he urged a campaign of nonviolence to resist abortion. It is startling but true that Jesse Jackson was among the first people to call for pro-life nonviolent action. But then he got politics and forgot all that unfashionable anti-abortion stuff, just walked away from it. He's not consistent and honest and gutsy about his principles. Further, we don't think he had any grasp of "nonviolence." He talked about it as if it's just a way to get good press. To be fair, if the only model you have for nonviolence is King, you are likely to think nonviolence is about good press, because King's work did indeed get good press, and the way we understand his work does blend the two. But they are not the same at all. If you think nonviolence is about good press, you understand neither nonviolence nor 21st century press.

Nonviolence without habitual respect for the law is a "Himalayan miscalculation"

In *The Story of My Experiments with Truth*, Gandhi asserts, "Before one can be fit for the practice of civil disobedience one must have rendered a willing and respectful obedience to the State laws." Someone who is committed to nonviolence as Gandhi understood it "accepts the laws of society intelligently and of his own free will, because he considers it to be his sacred duty to do so." Civil disobedience is not simply disregard for the laws that unite a civil society. "It is only when a person has thus obeyed the laws of society scrupulously that he is in a position to judge as to which particular laws are good and just and which unjust and iniquitous." Only then can a person claim the right to civil disobedience of certain laws in well-defined circumstances.

Gandhi said that his failure to observe this limitation, and to launch civil disobedience before the people had shown themselves to be properly qualified for it, was a mistake of "Himalayan magnitude."

Gandhi asserted that using civil disobedience too often cuts away the roots of society. The use of civil disobedience will be healthy and effective only if the activists generally conform to the law. Activists must be much more "civil" than "disobedient." Disobedience without civility and discipline and love is not admirable and useful; it's just destructive. (*Young India*, January 5, 1922)

It's gotta be respectful of opponents

If you opt for nonviolent action, you have got to study a foreign language, an alien culture, a new and startling vision and hope, aiming for a new global civilization.

Nonviolence is based firmly on an attitude toward our opponents. Love your enemies: this is not decorative, not optional, not some vague celestial aspiration: this is the solid core. Love: you want to be with them, you take great joy in their strengths and accomplishments, you seek out ways to cooperate when possible (while confronting when necessary), you put up with their attacks on you for many reasons, including because you understand and appreciate their loyalty to their friends.

Some ask, puffing smoke and snot: How can we have common ground with the satanic demonic Democratic pro-aborts? It's worthwhile to invest time in reading the *Compendium of the Social Doctrine of the Church*. Doctrine: that means the stuff that the Church holds and teaches. When Catholics get baptized, we declare – or our parents declare and we later affirm – that we hold what the Church teaches: that's doctrine. Doctrine is a hard word. The Catholic Church holds and teaches a large body of thought about justice. If you skim the *Compendium*, or even just check the table of contents, you can get a quick overview of Catholic doctrine regarding immigration, foreign aid, the wealth gap, labor, the environment, nuclear weapons and effective global authority (aka "world government"), poverty, education, human rights – as well as life and family issues. Many pro-life Catholics take a cafeteria approach; they are unapologetic systematic dissenters, taking what they like and ignoring the rest. But an honest examination reveals promptly that the Catholic Church has a long-standing global progressive pro-life perspective.

There's a detail that emerges from trying to think through the Church's teaching: immigration is emphatically not more important than abortion, but immigration policies are far more important to serious pro-lifers than the *Dobbs* decision. *Dobbs* could perhaps save thousands of children and families annually, and that's good. But a pro-life/pro-choice position on aid to pregnant and postpartum refugees could save hundreds of thousands of children from abortion, annually; that's good too. And a renewed pro-life/pro-choice initiative to resist forced abortion globally – partly by migration as a last resort – could protect several million babies and their families from abortion annually. Those two initiatives, which are far more effectively pro-life than *Dobbs*, begin with respect for our opponents. So we really must stop calling them nasty names; it's not just a bad habit, contrary to the teaching of the Lord; it's also murderous. We need pro-choice allies! *Tens of millions of unborn children need pro-lifers to be willing to cooperate with our opponents!*

The flat refusal to cooperate with our opponents is totally incompatible with nonviolence. Nonviolence seeks out areas of cooperation, with unswerving hope and determination. Cooperation in political matters is not the same thing as nonviolent action, but it is part of a nonviolent campaign. The desire to cooperate when possible – balanced with the decision to confront when necessary – is obviously an aspect of love, and it is foundational in true nonviolence.

Nonviolent action is not magic. You don't just get arrested and then watch the world change. You befriend your opponents, and then suffer with the vulnerable – and *then* people who have come to know you and trust you are disturbed in their hearts by your imprisonment. If we are perceived by our opponents as rotten ignorant obstructionist jackasses, they are not challenged by our willingness to go to jail. On the contrary, they are relieved, even delighted! They don't search their consciences to understand us, or to see how to help us – and then maybe begin to re-think those funny tiny things we claim that we love, those fetuses that cause so much perplexity. No! If we are despicable, they search the laws to figure out how to keep us where they think we belong. Nonviolence touches hearts *after* respect and affection soften hearts.

Nellie Gray, the founder of the March for Life, repeated for decades that "we do not negotiate with baby-killers." That's fun to say, I guess; but it's immensely destructive. We can't negotiate about when and where to kill innocent people, but we certainly can negotiate with anyone about *how* to protect vulnerable people, including pregnant refugees and women facing coercive abortion.

King says that a campaign of nonviolence cannot begin action until the participants have purified themselves. "Purify": whazzat? Some kind of sex thing, or maybe some kind of no-sex thing? No! It's about many things, but especially about our failures to love our opponents! Your actions aren't nonviolent if you say please and thank you; they are becoming nonviolent when you love your opponents. That's the true meaning of purity of heart.

Jesus says that we should not focus on external and ritual purity, but rather on what is within; and if we give alms, everything will be clean or kosher or pure (*katharos*) for us (Lk 11:41). St. James writes that religion that is pure (*katharos*) is caring for orphans and widows (James 1:27). When Jesus talked about being attached to the true vine – to himself – he said that the Father prunes us so we can bear more fruit (Jn 15:1-3); the fruit that we are pruned to produce, and commanded to produce, is that we love one another (Jn 15:17). This is "purity." So Rev. King, talking about nonviolent activists who need to "purify" themselves, is not talking about chastity; he is using the word the same way Jesus and his disciples did. In the New Testament, references to purity are about loving service, not about chastity. We're not against chastity, but *"purity of heart" is not a synonym for chastity*. We need God's help to love as we should – that is, to love with the Lord's all-embracing love, to love our enemies. A campaign of nonviolence can't launch properly until the participants pray and meditate and fast and *focus on loving our opponents* and renew our determination to do so – and that's what King was talking about.

I admired Nellie Gray, but she invited pro-lifers to demonize our opponents. King, following the teaching of the Lord, demanded the opposite, that we figure out how to love them. A campaign of pro-life nonviolence must respectfully discard Gray's advice and embrace King's.

Nonviolence has the power to end abortion – not to tinker like *Dobbs*, but to end it. It is the only plausible way forward. Please listen, friend: we are not changing the topic or fuzzing the agenda when we talk about immigration, for example. Even if we are sharply and almost exclusively focused on abortion, still we must find ways to work with our opponents – to love and appreciate and promote what is good in their lives. And immigration offers substantial common ground. The search for areas of agreement and cooperation is basic, rock-solid deeply foundational, in pro-life nonviolence!

Children are dying. So act, don't just talk. Women are being exploited, shoved deeper and deeper into traps. So act, don't just talk. But if we want to be effective, we have to expand our understanding of our role, our goal, our call. If we focus on defeating our enemies, we can slip easily from fighting Planned Parenthood to fighting Democrats (including me [JCOK] and leftists like me [EK]), and even get around to considering pregnant moms as potential or current enemies. We are not 100% sure we're not overlooking a case somewhere, but we're pretty sure that pro-lifers in the Midwest are working to send a post-abortion mom to jail *for the first time in American history*. Before *Roe v. Wade*, abortion was illegal – but abortionists and not women went to jail. American judges never, ever – not once, as far as we know – jailed post-abortion women. Until very recently, every pro-lifer saw women facing an unplanned pregnancy as victims with the threatened children. That's changing, as we watch. The hardness of "pro-life" hearts is shocking beyond belief. Don't do that! Focus on protection, on love – loving children, which has got to include loving their moms, and then searching for other allies in the struggle to serve. Pro-choicers have often been our allies, and must be again – not in everything we do, but in much of it.

Nonviolence. Love children, and act. Love pregnant women, and act carefully. Love our opponents, and act effectively. Nonviolently.

Nonviolence. Study, pray or meditate, admit and repair what we have done wrong, love in mind and heart and word and act. That's the hard daily work. (Prison: that's just M&Ms in the frosting.)

Effective and global

Pro-life nonviolent action (PNA) is multi-faceted. It's often an actual effective rescue. It's obedience to the Biblical injunction to rescue those doomed to die. It's an act of solidarity with a child. It's an extension of sidewalk counseling. It can be part of an educational campaign. It can be used to support a political effort. Most Americans who looked briefly at the work of Martin Luther King see civil disobedience as a way to get publicity. True, true, all true at least in part. But let us add a facet. *A campaign of pro-life nonviolent action is the solid foundation for the whole pro-life movement. This is a way to change society, throughout the nation and the world.* Many pro-lifers followed Trump because they were desperate to see success in the only strategy they had ever known for ending abortion: they were desperate! But that desperate dash for the goal line was a failure. A campaign of nonviolence is the way forward – to protect children one by one, and also to end abortion, nationally and globally. This is the alternative to the Trump dream – honest, and global, and hopeful.

Let us re-word that. This is not *an* alternative; this is the *only* alternative (other than surrender). In fact, this is now, and always has been, the only way forward for the pro-life movement. I pray that the fraud of the Trump years will indeed offer pro-lifers something valuable: a wake-up call. May Trump's emptiness and violence finally wake us up to listen to the clear teaching of common sense and history and the Church – and finally cut us loose from cheap solutions and finally let us see the true and only way forward!

Nonviolence is not just one *tactic* among many; it is rather an embracing *strategy*, and it is the *only* one that offers hope. The 20th century offered a huge increase in possibilities for violence: nukes. But the century also offered an alternative that is as powerful as nukes and as effective as any war has ever been: nonviolence.

But nonviolence has its own methods and measures and training and discipline. If you say you are embracing nonviolence but then despise and assault your enemies, you are deluded or lying. If you refuse to embrace the good in your enemies, you have already failed and need to start all over. If you mix violence and nonviolence, one foot planted tentatively in each boat, open-minded and pro-choice about methods, you cannot prepare properly and you will certainly fail.

I [JCOK] was up and running, promoting nonviolence across the country in 1980, when Reagan was elected President and 12 new pro-life Senators were elected. I was writing for *National Right to Life News* when the Republicans and pro-life allies launched a new administration. I was first to report it when David Stockman, the Director of Reagan's Office of Management and Budget, said that the administration would prioritize the economy over right to life matters. I covered the struggle over Sandra Day O'Connor's confirmation – when the years of work to bring in a pro-life administration produced a pro-abortion Justice. I was in the National Right to Life Committee office when Rep. Henry Hyde explained to us why Reagan appointed her. Hyde said that Reagan assured him that she was pro-life; he asked her about it, and she said she was "personally opposed to abortion." Hyde pressed Reagan: "Did you ask her about *Roe v. Wade*? Reagan responded, "*Roe v. Wade*? What's that?" I was there when the disillusionment set in, and many pro-lifers gave up on the political struggle and turned to activism. I knew that activists were split on whether to turn to violence, and I helped to launch and lead the alternative, a nonviolent effort that was small but that inspired sit-ins in every state in the nation, 50 out of 50 plus DC.

Nonviolence was the right way to go, but it was *also an alternative to violence* – and we needed that.

It is catastrophically different today. At first glance, it seems that the pro-life movement is flexing muscle in the wake of the *Dobbs* decision. However, if you look a little more closely, you see that the movement has almost peaked, far short of our stated political and legislative goal. More than a dozen states have banned abortion and a couple dozen more will likely do so. But then what? Well, then it's over, for the people who put all their eggs in one basket, implementing the ancient NRLC strategy, educate-to-legislate-to-total-protection. Some states will *not* act to protect unborn children in the foreseeable future. So abortion will remain available in the US, for anyone anywhere. Pro-choicers will be deeply outraged that many women will have to travel for some hours to get an abortion. But when reality finally takes hold, pro-lifers will also be deeply upset – because any woman, anywhere in the country, can get an abortion if she can travel. And then there will be violence from "pro-lifers."

Overall, surgical abortion within the US may have declined about five percent since *Dobbs*. We think abortion stats are highly unreliable, but birthrate stats are probably reliable, and the birthrate has increased slightly. See, for example, a study reported by NPR, finding that in a one-year period starting some months after *Dobbs*, after some states had banned abortion, births were up about 30,000 for the nation, which does not prove but does suggest that there were likely 30,000 abortions averted.

Each birth was a success with eternal ramifications. But for decades, the legal strategy shoved nonviolence aside, in order to bring about an end to all abortions, "not just a few itty-bitty little babies" (in the words of one NRLC leader). Now, that strategy has run almost its full course; some state battles remain. It's mostly over, and it's five percent successful – and even that limited success is fragile.

When pro-lifers finally admit that their (our) long-term strategy to end abortion by changing the law has been a near-total failure, peaking at about five percent of the stated goal, there will be trouble of some kind. It will be like the 1980s, when pro-lifers expected Reagan to act decisively to end abortion, and were extremely disappointed when he failed and appointed Sandra Day O'Connor to the Supreme Court. But focus carefully on a huge difference between then and now. In the 1980s, there were pro-life nonviolent voices everywhere. At all pro-life events in the 1980s, there were people on the fringes if not in the middle of the meeting urging nonviolence. That is gone, almost entirely. Today, at all pro-life events, there are people on the fringes if not in the middle of the meeting talking about the Second Amendment. Sure, there are a few voices here and there among pro-lifers calling for something they label "nonviolence," but they are not referring to a principle like Gandhi's teaching; they want good manners.

Gandhi is out; guns are in. That's a change – and activism of some kind is coming soon to a theater near you. I [JCOK] expect pro-lifers to shift to activism in 2024 and 2025, but I do not see any moderating forces among us. We will soon see what happens when the Second Amendment meets *Dobbs*. Fortunately, most pro-lifers have been slow to figure out that *Dobbs* isn't magic; but when they do face reality, what will happen? I expect shooting and bombing, following the hard steel path shown by Jim Kopp and others.

Given the threat, I think it's urgent for intelligent people to take steps now. Civility matters. Rebuilding relationships with Democrats, almost as if we believed that they are actually fully human, is urgent. We will build a strong national (and international) campaign of pro-life nonviolent action, or we will watch "pro-life" violence spin out of control.

Calling the cops

It seems to me [JCOK] worthwhile to ask pro-lifers whether they would call the cops about a "pro-life" bomber. It would be worthwhile to collect public declarations from anti-violent pro-lifers that we will be proactive about policing our own, stopping assassins and bombers. Mao said that guerrillas could swim among the people like a fish in the sea. That sounds cute and lovely, perhaps. But me? I'm no part of that sea. Unequivocally, I condemn "pro-life" violence, and I will do whatever I can to prevent it. And since I can't stop "pro-life" violence myself, I'll call the cops when I see it.

I am puzzled when people claim they are committed to nonviolence, but they are opposed to calling the cops when they see violence that they can't stop themselves. Sometimes people aren't *opposed* to calling the cops, just *conflicted and indecisive* – which comes to the same thing.

There are some principled anarchists who wouldn't call the cops to prevent violence against themselves, people like Dan Berrigan and Mubarak Awad (and EK). They are not the problem. The problem is huge numbers of pro-lifers who certainly will call the police to protect themselves – but not to protect an abortionist from assassination.

There are some activists with experience in maintaining moral law and order without summoning help from the city or county or state. I have a great deal of respect for that, and Gandhi supported such community-based order among his followers. But I note that even Gandhi spoke about how his people could handle crimes against property – but didn't give examples of how they responded to crimes against life. Pro-lifers have had killers in our midst, claiming to be completely "pro-life."

I reject the political strategy, *and* I oppose violence. That narrows real strategic options to one.

Not calling the cops

I [EK] avoid calling the cops whenever possible. This is a commitment I made after facing police brutality during Black Lives Matter events. My experience shaped my perspective that bringing the police into the picture frequently results in more violence, not in de-escalation. I saw my comrades de-escalate violence in our community and came to believe that we, everyday civilians, have the power to keep us safe. Even Gandhi spoke against calling the cops:

> "A *satyagrahi* [practitioner of nonviolence] will not report a criminal to the police. He will not try to ride two horses at a time, viz., to pretend to follow the law of *satyagraha* [nonviolence] while at the same time seeking police aid ... A reformer cannot afford to be an informer."

JCOK: The quote from Gandhi is valid and challenging, but he was not an absolutist about this. He supported the British decision to go to war against Hitler. The context in which he opposed calling the police concerned property damage, not killing helpless people. Still, you are right to see him as an ally in the struggle to develop ways to de-escalate from violent confrontation without calling the police.

How we can best prevent violence is to remain vigilant for violent sentiments arising amongst our people and intervene to diffuse them. We must also proactively foster a commitment to nonviolence in such a way that it is not seen as a tactic or strategy, but as a lifestyle and creed. Study nonviolence. Discuss it. Write about it. Sing about it. Reflect on it. Pledge to it. Hang it on the wall. Tell your friends about it. Give frequent reminders.

When I say *we keep us safe*, "us" means everyone, including abortionists. It is the duty of a pro-lifer to protect everyone from violence, as we must love our enemies. So John poses a challenging question: if I got intel that someone was planning to commit violence against an abortionist, what would I do, if not inform the police? I don't think there's a one-size-fits-all answer, and that each case requires nuance. Maybe that's a cop-out. But here's a general outline of what I might try to do:

First, I would inform the abortionist so they could take measures to protect themselves. I expect the abortionist will make a report to the police. Does this defeat the point of me *not* calling the police in the first place? Pragmatically yes, but it keeps my integrity intact. I can't control how others will react.

Then, I would consider the capacity of my community to provide defense. We might suggest to the abortionist to arrange a nightwatch in collaboration with local pro-choicers, or a marshal service to guard them. I don't foresee them accepting these offers, but it's our duty to provide them if requested.

Then, I would make attempts to talk down the potential violator, or to detain them with trusted comrades if the situation has already escalated. Again, we might arrange a watch to monitor and deter them. After some time has passed, we check on them periodically. We have to love them too, while maintaining appropriate boundaries.

Last resort – I concede, I would call the police if I could see no other viable strategy to address the situation. But I encourage us to try to imagine a world without police and incarceration in their current forms, just as I encourage everyone to imagine a world beyond abortion. It just requires imagination, courage, and love to see that we have more real options than violence.

A New Way

It is our conviction that the slaughter of unborn children is the worst violence in the history of the world. It is our conviction that this slaughter can and will be ended, although God only knows when. It is our conviction that the slaughter must be ended by coordinated and intelligent and loving action, not by random acts of kindness. And it is our conviction that humanity already has in hand models for how to go about this; we have seen campaigns of nonviolence bring about huge changes.

Pro-lifers started such a campaign, but leaders refused to learn from their predecessors, and made mistakes that disrupted and ended the effort. Can anyone sweep the glowing embers together and rekindle this fire?

The whole pro-life movement is in flux now. The catastrophic embrace of the Trump-Court strategy – including systematic polarization of the nation and a savage renunciation of all things demonic/Democratic – has almost run its course, and now (2024) seven state elections have made clear how counter-productive that strategy was. Some people will double down: there is no cure for stupidity. Others will walk away in disgust or turn to violence (recall St. Peter in Gethsemane). But some will look for a new way and may recall how Mary Magdalene's response differed from Peter's. Some people might even read the teaching of John Paul II in *The Gospel of Life* and the *Compendium* – not excerpts and slogans, but the whole encyclical. Then something effective can emerge.

Modeling constructive criticism

A candid analysis of a nonviolent action should be standard for activists. It's an obvious tool and should have been common all along; but it hasn't been. People who risk their freedom to help others, and who are rewarded for their integrity by social isolation and bitter denunciations need simple support! But a healthy movement, to grow, needs to offer support and also candid feedback. So here goes.

This is a critique of a rescue in 2020 as shown on various videotapes at trial in October 2023. I [JCOK] offer this as an example – not because this specific sit-in was particularly problematic. We need to critique our actions, carefully and openly and bluntly. We need to candid with ourselves – and God and others – about what we are trying to do, and about what we do wrong. Candor can sting, but we need it to learn. And we can be candid if we are working together as a community called by God. There were some things that happened that shouldn't happen again, and we need an open discussion of them. Open discussion clarifies what we mean by "nonviolence."

The rescue in 2020 was at an abortion clinic in Washington DC. The rescuers were tried and convicted in 2023, and sentenced in 2024. Their determination to protect the helpless is an inspiring story, and their sacrifices were huge and laudable. May we all aspire to do a fraction of what they did! I offer a critique, but it's a critique of heroic action by amazing people.

They were all charged with violating the Freedom of Access to Clinic Entrances, or FACE, a Federal offense created during the Clinton administration, with a one-year penalty. Additionally, they were charged with conspiracy – planning a "crime" together, like all people who engage in civil disobedience – which carries ten years.

The leader of the action was Lauren Handy. She chose the site, because the abortionist there was engaged in particularly gruesome late-term abortions. She suspected that some of the abortions at the Washington Surgi-Clinic were in fact infanticide, and urged the police to examine the bodies that she recovered in 2022 from the waste stream after abortions there. Her request was completely and consistently refused. She had some large bodies of babies killed there; that evidence of horrific crimes was ignored, except that Lauren was arrested and smeared for days, charged with illegal possession of human remains. Those charges were dropped. In 2023, she was convicted of violating FACE, and of conspiracy; she was sentenced to 57 months in prison.

Joan Andrews Bell was the best known of the rescuers. Her three years in prison in the 1980s galvanized the rescue movement. Various men got credit for building that movement; but the real leaders were women, especially Joan. In 2024, she was sentenced to 27 months in prison.

Will Goodman was the most articulate rescuer. He too had a record – though it was not nearly as long as Joan's! His words before sentencing were inspiring. He was sentenced to 27 months in prison.

John Hinshaw has a wife and family who will suffer in his absence. He is easy to overlook because he is content to let his actions and his demeanor speak for him. When he does look up, his eyes are full of intelligent joy. When he speak, it's worth listening carefully. He was sentenced to 21 months in prison.

Heather Idoni is a gentle person active in a variety of charitable works. For example, in the years just before she was imprisoned, she was collecting and shipping packages of medical supplies to Ukrainian soldiers. Her open-hearted plea to protect unborn children – seen at her trial – was poignant, unforgettable. She was sentenced to 24 months in prison.

Herb Geraghty is a quiet person with an unassuming air – but he is a capable organizer, the executive director of Rehumanize International. At the March for Life, his organization has provided space for atheists and non-binary people who might find large parts of the pro-life movement to be culturally distant. He was sentenced to 27 months in prison.

Jonathan Darnell is an intense man who cries out for the churches to act with determination, to "get more serious" about the deaths of children in our midst. He has worked for years to show bloody photos to as many people as possible, urging action. He filmed much of the rescue in 2020. He was sentenced to 34 months in prison.

Jean Marshall is a determined woman who does not hesitate to speak her mind. She participated in the lock & block part of the rescue. She was sentenced to 24 months in prison.

Jay Smith has a family who depend on him, and he was not in a position to risk years in prison. He participated in life-saving action, but took steps to minimize his time away from home. That is, he plea-bargained. He pled guilty, and was sentenced to ten months in prison.

Paulette Harlow, Jean's sister, participated in the rescue in 2020, but between the rescue and the trial, her health deteriorated. She was convicted, and was sentenced to 24 months in prison.

These ten people risked their freedom to protect children and to offer support to women who felt trapped. They deserve the thanks and praise of all decent people who understand what abortion is. However, if pro-life nonviolent action is going to spread, not disappear, we need clear and direct examination of the shortcomings in their heroic work. We need radical candor! But honest observers will be clear: this is a discussion of mistakes made by admirable people. Pro-lifers should all be deeply inspired by their loving acts and respectful of their intentions, even as we dissect their mistakes.

Physical force

The scrum at the door was a test of plain muscle, not spiritual force. If a rescue becomes a wrestling match, we lose, 100% guaranteed, even if we win the match and open the door. This action, from the very first seconds, was a contest of physical strength.

EK: That's not what the participants told me happened. The scrum at the door was caused by patients pushing past the rescuers, causing them to tumble into the waiting room.

JCOK: I saw the footage, and that account seems dubious based on what I saw. But I acknowledge there are different interpretations of the videotape.

The secrecy functioned, as usual, to keep secrets from participants, not opponents. Will didn't know anyone was bringing locks. Are you going to do that again?

The shouting included some non-rescuers. But the rescuers could be heard above the din – a verbal scrum to match the rugby scrum at the door. I don't know about you, but I don't think carefully when there's shouting, especially when I'm the one who's shouting.

Videotape of the event recorded a male voice taking command firmly, loudly. It was pretty amazing to hear a male shouting in the clinic. Is there a better way to make sure a woman remembers why she's there in the first place than having some man try to take control, shouting? It's hard to think of a better way to persuade women to get the damn abortion done asap.

Some (not all) of the rescuers in the clinic radiated a sense of entitlement. Yes, I am quite sure God invited them to this action. But no, I don't think they arrived as conquerors. It was a very strange vibe, and the loud patient picked up on it.

Someone was shouting about hell. I doubt it was a patient. Probably not clinic staff either. I am pretty sure it was fun to shout, but is there any reason to believe it was helpful at that moment in that place?

If you shout, what people hear is just crap. If you shout about Jesus, you make Jesus sound like crap. Don't do that.

Tone!

The shouting was bad, but what was equally problematic was what didn't happen. The failure even to try to *control the tone* was a related but separate problem. Controlling the tone as well as you as you can is fundamental, and I couldn't see any serious effort to control the tone. If I get in your face, turn purple, and scream that you better take the thousand dollars I'm giving you, you will probably refuse. Tone trumps words. If you lose control of the tone, your message is gone too.

There was some noise that made you think someone might be trying to sing. Wow. Music calms the savage breast unless it's repulsive. But a clinic is not a place to practice. Practice ahead of time, and nail it when lives are at stake.

Good music takes practice. The lack of practice was obvious, and insulting.

At the trial, there was no prayer or music in the halls. Lawyers set the tone (whisper, whisper, pompous, important, power), and defined the parameters of success (get out of jail free). Amazing! Of course there was some resistance to prayer and music. So work it out, find a way, compromise a little, sing antiphonally and hum responses, move away a little, sing in the elevator, dance slowly from one small choir to another, go up or down a floor, go outside, mix it with prose. Don't just give up!

Prayer versus politics and law

The lack of prayer or music was related to tone. Again: the failure is one thing, and the nonsense that filled the hole is another. The tone of the news event (press conference?) post-trial noise was shrill, confrontational, boring, predictable, a repulsive caricature of a pro-life speech. It looked like a script written by Planned Parenthood to mock us.

Defining success is always a struggle – indeed, one might argue that it is the most important struggle in human life. Is heaven victory, or a million dollars: choose! So struggle to define it. For many lawyers most of the time, success is easy to define: you win or lose depending on the verdict. Activists should be clear: solidarity and nonviolence have a totally different approach, worlds away from the verdict! Success for an activist is, for example: we stand in solidarity, visibly and tangibly, with dying children and trapped women: *success!* Before God, I am ready to be a calm light in a sordid and noisy world: *success!* I recall that my Lord was arrested, humiliated, tortured, and executed – and I hear him invite me to follow: *success!* We are the successors of nonviolent heroes: *success!* Every child anywhere who lives and breathes is a pro-life *success!* This immensely important truth was not clear at the rescue, nor in court.

Total lack of dialogue with opponents

Nonviolence is meaningless outside your relationship with your opponents. There was zero evidence of any relationship with the abortionist or clinic staff in the event, and again in court.

Politics can be like the law, with winners and losers, and with each side struggling to beat and defeat and subdue and maybe obliterate opponents. Politics can be the art of the possible, operating with a determination to find common ground and/or acceptable compromises. But in the era of Trump, all that lady-like politesse has become ancient history. Nonviolence is different; it ceases to exist when you demonize your opponents.

It troubles me when I hear pro-lifers asserting confidently that the abortion movement is driven by money – presumably, as I hear the criticism, more than other industries. For sure, there's money there. But I think the driving forces include an ideology – eugenics or population control – and a defense of personal sexual habits, or plain lust, including the "contraceptive mentality" against "repressive Victorian hang-ups" or some such. And once abortion has taken root in our society, there's another force that maintains it: simple loyalty. It's deeply troubling to me when I listen to pro-lifers – friends and colleagues for decades – who seem to have zero appreciation of the huge value of loyalty to women in distress – a concern that we share with many of our opponents, although we differ in extraordinarily significant ways about how to help the distressed.

"I can't even imagine doing that!" Usually, when people assert this abject failure to understand something, they move promptly from ignorance to lofty indignant speechifying. Weird. If you can't imagine, let alone understand, shouldn't you shut up and listen? Our opponents *do* explain themselves – often clearly and honestly. Why do we dismiss their motives so fast, with such suspicion and hostility?

At court, one prosecutor was an aristocrat with his nose in the air. But a second prosecutor had a brief but cordial exchanges with anyone who approached him. Despite his open demeanor, he was demonized! Why?

The lack of training and prep

It was shocking to see the extent to which the lawyers shaped the perception of loss and victory.

I [JCOK] did not see or hear an articulate explanation of solidarity. This was particularly painful when Caroline D (a young woman who came to Washington to participate in the rescue, but then was convinced it was a mistake and testified for the prosecution) took a shot at it; she knew some things, but it was tantalizing rather than convincing. It is not surprising that she rejected the idea that she explained. (Joan Andrews Bell defended Caroline with joy and insight; that was true nonviolence, and it was inspiring. But Caroline's words didn't show a robust understanding.)

I did not hear any hint that it is not just legitimate but joyful when people ask, and demand a lived and visible response to their question: "Do you mean it when you say this is your brother/sister? Prove it." What an honor and privilege to be in a position to answer that question! The ten in prison answer that question with clarity, until pro-lifers start moaning and groaning and pleading for mercy *for adults*.

I was shocked to the core by the determination to focus on the evil done by evil-horrible-demonic Santangelo. Was that fundraising? A scramble for press? Honest shock, undigested? What in hell – speaking carefully and literally – what in hell was that all about? It's like showing up at Calvary and writing an article about Pontius Pilate.

The rescue participants included some elderly and relatively frail women. What a brave choice on their part! But having older women with brittle bones in your midst does require some planning and adjustment. The failure to work out ahead of time what they were doing there, and whether or how to protect them, was painful to see. A significant part of the history of American brutality has been built on the "need" to protect vulnerable women. That is, the KKK lynched black men and tortured and killed them – but tried to justify these crimes by explaining to themselves and others that they were preventing rape. No one was raping anyone at the abortion clinic, but there was a shoving match at the door: should a husky young man make sure the door wasn't crushed against elderly women? What was the plan? What did people expect? What was going on in the training? Again, the obvious total lack of training and community building was obvious.

A strong young man among the rescuers shoved open the door and shouted a lot, a domineering male presence and voice inside an abortion clinic. Dear Lord. But note well: his obvious and glaring mistakes were not just his fault. Where was his training? In addition, his friends now feel that loyalty means they have to defend him. But training can and indeed must include a different approach to mistakes. After his very costly errors, he should know with tranquil certainty that he still belongs within a community that forgives. Does he know, from the preparation for the action, that he is embraced by a community that loves him? If so, why does anyone feel any need to defend or cover up his errors? Training in nonviolence includes a commitment to repentance – personal and communal. We all make mistakes; we all see and understand our own and others' mistakes; we are ready to admit them and learn from them and forgive them and move on: this is fundamental in nonviolence, and in communal training!

Outside with cops, Lauren demonstrated that she knew what she was doing – but there was no spillover from her to others. Who was in charge? The lack of clear confident assertive leadership was so distressing!

Why in the world was Caroline D so malleable? Where was her training?

The lack of coordination was astounding. The sit-in looked like four separate efforts all mushed together. It wasn't any one of them; it was a mishmash of (1) evangelization, (2) nonviolence, (3) Red Rose, and (4) Jim Kopp lock-and-block.

Candor and satyagraha

How in the world did an FBI spy learn anything? Why wasn't everything in the open, so spying would be meaningless? What was being hidden? This is another Kopp legacy! Nonviolence does not need secrecy. When in doubt, run for the light! A relevant excerpt from Gandhi's *Non-Violence in Peace and War:*

> "No secret organization, however big, could do any good. Secrecy aims at building a wall of protection around you. *Ahimsa* [nonviolence] disdains all such protection. It functions open in the face of odds, the heaviest conceivable... They cannot be organized by other than open, truthful means."

Gandhi's word for nonviolence was *satyagraha*, which means the "Truth" and/or "Clinging to the Truth." The truth, in human experience, includes candor.

The speech to the press

The speeches – was that a press conference? – were defensive: we will prevail in the end despite this setback – that sort of stuff. What mind-boggling nonsense! A great victory at hand, labeled a defeat by the leaders. Again.

The proper assignment at a nonviolent press conference seems clear to me: make sure people understand what just happened. This is not about some adults who got screwed over; this is about children whose lives are of immense value. The world asks, are those dead things worth any fuss? And some wonderful people stood forth to say – in effect – unborn children were and are our brothers and sisters, and we stand in solidarity with them. We thank God for letting us share in their rejection, to some small extent. It is worth years of our lives – perhaps 10% of our lives pledged today – to recall and declare how precious these children were and are to us!

The world asks a question: is it true that unborn children are members of the family? The world is not sure, but pro-lifers stand forth to proclaim the truth. The world, unsure, demands proof from us that we mean what we say. We urge them to look at the obvious: the beginning is at the beginning, not at 12 or 15 or 24 weeks after the beginning. The world remains dubious and asks: do you really believe that? Pro-lifers answer yes. The world asks again, are you sure? Can we test you? And then the world tests us. Dear God, what an honor! A handful of people are asked: do you mean it? And the world watches the answer! What a great moment! A group of mature and holy adults declares, in bright bold living action: yes, they are worth any sacrifice.

But wait. What did they say? Their spokespeople said, "Oops. We got caught. Oops. We lost the trial. Oops. We will try to be brave and not discouraged. Oops. Maybe next time."

I [JCOK] could not believe it. Still, still, still – these generous and good people have no idea what they are doing. Prison is testimony to the truth. Giving one's life for an idea can be admirable, but today – even among devout Christians – one hears criticism of a "martyr complex." "Complex"? Was Jesus neurotic? Were all the apostles, and a large part of the Christian community for three centuries – all suffering from mental illness? Muslims maintain some respect for martyrdom, even though they, like other religious communities, have to figure out how to respond to some crazies in their midst whose martyrdom may indeed reveal an unbalanced mind. But pro-lifers: have we lost track of the immense power of self-sacrifice? Martyrdom and prison are – let me be careful here: they *can* be – precious gifts from a loving God.

What can be done now? Once people lay hold of a false narrative, and suffer for it, it is almost impossible to persuade them to let it go, to try again and do it right.

What went well

I was proud to know the people who acted with courage and peace, even joy. Heather's simplicity was so inspiring. John and Will, in their calm, lifted my heart. Lauren was so good in her outreach to the cops. I didn't see as clearly what others were doing: my apologies for that. But I thank God for their courageous sacrifice!

This group needs prep, study, training, and honest feedback. They looked like politicians playing Activism. The gentle crucified Lord will teach us all to do better than that. May his name be praised forever.

Training for pro-life nonviolence

This is a sketch, based on some of the training offered by pro-life nonviolent activists in decades past. Different groups will train differently, but if you start with an outline, that helps.

A good training program for pro-life nonviolent action should take some weeks and weekends. Community-building is not optional or decorative: people involved need to spend time getting to know each other – not just in jail, but before the action. This should include reflecting together on some lessons, beginning with Scripture. Starting with the Bible shoves the group towards religion, and towards Christianity, and some will see that as a problem. It does pose challenges, but if Gandhi the Hindu can draw lessons from Jesus, you can too.

The Scripture readings, discussed together, should include:

- the four songs of the suffering servant in Isaiah
- the Sermon on the Mount
- numerous psalms and at least one entire Gospel

Prayer together should include the Rosary, even if the group is half Protestant and 10 percent atheist. Entry level: the Rosary calms people, a 15-minute familiar buzz. Next level: the Rosary is a good way to re-center in prayer together, focusing together on various incidents in the life of Jesus and the Church. Next: Asking Mary for help is a good idea. It's problematic for some Protestants, so participants should work out a list of music that Protestants can sing while Catholics do their ten-Hail-Mary thing. For example, "Lord, Prepare me to be a sanctuary" is a good musical accompaniment to the first mystery of the Rosary.

Singing together, with accompaniment and also a capella, is not decorative or optional. It strengthens resolve. It touches the heart along with the mind. Music intensifies prayer, of course, but it also calms crowds – unless the music is horrible. Pray together and sing together – and get good. Taizé offers a pile of ideas.

Activists need some of Gandhi's thought. The movie *Gandhi* is historical fiction, but it does help to get a handle on what he intended to do. Thomas Merton's introduction to Gandhi (*Gandhi on Non-Violence*, edited by Merton) is excellent. Get yourself a copy.

For groups committed to secularism, Merton's selections can stand in as your "sacred" text. Reflect on passages from the five sections (including "The Spiritual Dimensions" – discuss together how it is applicable to each participant) and draw lessons. Pick a short excerpt, memorize it, and repeat it 50 times to drill it into memory – the idea is to make it a mantra, something you can repeat absentmindedly to self-soothe under pressure. You must also foster a sense of duty and obedience; make "bravery consists in dying, not in killing" your group motto. And then pick some songs you can sing together; Terrisa Bukovinac's "Pro-Life Revolution" and Kristin Turner's "One Eye Open" are a good base for your repertoire.

You need Rev. Martin Luther King's thought, but don't dream of using what others say about him; get his own writing! Don't get censored like the memorial that glosses over Jesus and nonviolence.

To explain the history and philosophy of pro-life nonviolent action, participants should read a book written specifically for this task: *Emmanuel, Solidarity: God's Act, Our Response*, by JCOK. Get it, read it. It has three parts, and you want to read each part, and wrestle with the ideas. No one on earth – no one, not even the author – agrees with everything in it. But it grapples with the right topics and offers an abundance of insight.

Preparation must include some contact with:

- whoever offers pregnancy aid near the abortion clinic where you're going
- someone who can explain post-abortion counseling, and
- the police, whose day you're about to make very difficult

- Abortion staff might not want to say hello, but you must try, and try again, and again. Make sure they have a good opportunity to understand you. Build a relationship as well as you can, with mutual trust and affection.
- Same with the escorts. Immediately post-*Dobbs*, most groups in the nation have a policy against contact; never ever let go of the struggle to get around that inhuman and dehumanizing policy.

The training session the weekend or night before action should include:

- prayer, meditation, and music
- some reflection recalling carefully what you are planning
- some role play, covering:
  - how to enter,
  - how to act inside,
  - how to converse and how not to,
  - how to respond when you are insulted,
  - how to respond when you are attacked physically,
  - how to respond when others are insulted or attacked.

Everyone needs to speak up and/or act out in this part. You must hear each activist explain what they will do when attacked, so you don't interfere and screw it up. The most common reason pro-lifers turn to violence during an action is that they are defending each other, especially men defending women and the young defending the elderly. Work this out ahead of time!

Figure out your rules for touching each other. You shouldn't be shoving anyone around, but you are likely to get shoved, and bounce off other people. Talk it through ahead of time, and don't even think about suing each other.

It is impossible to plan for everything, but talk through some problems. Review expectations for arrests, charges, removal, booking, jail, court procedures, possible penalties. Talking it through is obviously helpful for the specific situations you deal with, but –

more importantly – it makes clear how your group will handle problems in general. Who prays? Who leads? Who advises? Who calms? Who has trouble? How do you decide what to do with unforeseen problems?

You simply cannot have a peaceful action without clear leadership – making decisions, not suggestions.

Set the tone! Communication in crisis is 90% nonverbal. Tone is a major part of the task of saving lives. Think hard about how to set a tone, maintain a tone, recover a tone. Your peaceful presence may be life-saving.

One of the most troublesome aspects of an action, often, is that the people risking arrest may be calm and collected, at peace with God and themselves and their immediate surroundings, while people outside or watching are frustrated and worried and angry. The tone outside may war against the tone inside – among pro-lifers! Be aware of this challenge, and let the people risking arrest set the tone. This will be hard! Obviously you don't want shouting inside; you don't want it outside either. Empower your musicians, and use them. This dynamic starts at least the evening before the action, during the training – or maybe at the beginning of your weeks or months of training.

Begin with prayer and meditation and probably music, and pause for prayer and meditation and probably music, and end with prayer and meditation and probably music.

Court

What a gift it is to get arrested and prosecuted! Jesus was not indulging in loopy poetry nor pointing to Paradise when he talked about imprisonment. He said, "Blessed are they who are persecuted for the sake of justice, for theirs is the kingdom of heaven." The kingdom of heaven is not simply otherworldly; it reaches back into the world of time and space that we all inhabit. We can taste it now, get hints now. And of the beatitudes in his sermon, this is the only one that he stops to gnaw on a little, giving details: "Blessed are you when they insult you and persecute you and utter every kind of evil against you because of me. Rejoice and be glad, for your reward will be great in heaven. Thus they persecuted the prophets who were before you." Yes, he puts the reward in the future; but he invites and even demands that we step into that future right now – rejoice and be glad *now*. (Mt 5:10-12)

Note that Jesus does not offer specific advice about what you should say, or what legal strategy to adopt; but he is clear and forceful about the tone that we should set.

Jesus gave clear and explicit instructions about court. Don't worry about what you are to say; the Spirit and intuition will give you words when the time comes. That doesn't mean don't prepare! But it does mean that preparation for court might *completely ignore the agenda set by the court*. Were you there, were you asked to leave, was the person who asked you to leave properly authorized, did this happen in my jurisdiction, did you punch or coerce anyone, did you conspire? Yes yes yes yes no yes – now let's talk about something real. Proper preparation for court is simply prayer: teach me, Lord, to do your will. For the secular, a simple meditation: I will act in service of love, not fear.

Your sacrifice is testimony that the life of a child is precious. Do not let others dilute that clear message. If you are jailed, that's not a mistake; it's clear testimony. You can't go to jail by accident if you go on purpose; avoid it if the opportunity to go free is handed to you, but expect to go to jail and embrace the invitation to give clear testimony.

Lawyers have their own definition of success, and their own agenda based on that definition. Do not accept that! It completely distorts your clear testimony.

The whole court phenomenon is intimidating. Feel the pressure, but then dismiss it. Just dust in a black bag, on a stool behind a ridiculous desk: do not be afraid. Give witness to the value of a child's life.

Pray. Meditate. Sing. Don't play the legal mumbo-jumbo game. Be respectful of the people who are trying to hold society together: God bless them! But they should not be wasting your time. Give your witness, and don't sweat it.

Prison

Study strangers and alienation, and then especially the history and theology of the scapegoat. And remember to pray for others, diligently. Contemplate the humanity of your enemies. If you are imprisoned, you are not a passive victim; you are a pioneer. Your vocation is almost the same vocation that monks had – not exactly, but a lamb of God. Your job is to be a cycle-breaker.

(I [JCOK] should be honest and clear here: I have experienced jail, but not prison. My words about prison are limited; I am ignorant.)

In consideration of prison, intergenerational organizing becomes essential: who is most available to put their entire lives on hold out of love for their preborn siblings? Usually, it's young adults, the elderly, and anyone who isn't currently supporting a nuclear family. So, the young and the old are prime candidates to take on the risks of rescue, and to weather the consequences together.

Strategic tenacity

It makes sense to count the cost. Most rescue leaders insist that the laws passed in response to Operation Rescue in the 1980s and the current use of conspiracy charges to make it hard to risk arrest to save lives. May I offer two vignettes, some philology, and three prayers?

Joe Wall was a great rescuer from Philadelphia – faithful when there were crowds and faithful when he was alone. He told a story about picketing alone outside a Philly area hospital, in a heavy snowfall. Alone: what's the point? He remembered picketing there then because it was so bleak; but he also remembered it because of an event years later. He was picketing again, and a young woman ran up to him and embraced him and introduced herself. She was a delighted parent. She told Joe that she was inside that abortion clinic, minutes from ending a difficulty in her life, and looked out the window. Down below, there was a guy walking up and down in the heavy falling snow, with a sign. She saw him stop and kneel down in the snow, and thought that if he was willing to go to all that trouble for her child, she should too. So she left, and had a baby, and raised the child, and she wanted to thank Joe. Thank God, but Joe too!

You do not know – you cannot know, and perhaps you should not know – when your work has an impact.

Carol Crossed was (and may still be) the major funder of leftwing pro-life work. I remember writing to Cardinal Bernardin shortly before he died with a question about funding to promote the "seamless garment." My question was not where to find funding, but more simply whether such funding existed, as far as he knew, aside from Carol Crossed. He responded simply: no. Carol was and is amazing. She's not all that wealthy, but she is all that generous. One year, she organized a national conference for Prolifers for Survival, which later morphed into the Consistent Life Network. Dan Berrigan – a Jesuit who had been in prison for years for nonviolent resistance to war, one of the nation's foremost peace activists – was among the speakers. She wanted the conference to include nonviolent action at an abortion clinic, and – near the end of the event – asked me how to do it. I said that there was still time, but she would have to take a risk. She should announce at the Friday evening session that on Saturday morning she – she alone if necessary – was going to sit in the door of the abortion clinic some miles away. If she announced it, people would join her – probably. But she had to step out, alone and vulnerable. So she did, and people did join her, including Dan Berrigan. One of the most solid planks in the fragile bridge between pro-lifers and peace activists was Berrigan's decision. And he acted because Carol stepped out, alone and scared.

Again: you do not know – you cannot know, and perhaps you should not know – when your work will have an impact.

Why should we ever take risks, when the results may be small and the price may be high? *(Uh-oh. An English teacher is gonna answer, and it's gonna be weird.)* The word *why* in English is ambiguous in a way that is worth pondering. Everything that happens in the universe unfolds within a chain of causality – this happens and so that happens and so the next thing happens. The word in English looks both ways along the chain – back towards causes and forward towards intended results. Consider, for clarifying contrast, French and Spanish: the equivalent words are *pourquoi* and *por qué* – for what? In those languages, the word tilts towards the future; the question about why suggests that we undertake an action in order to achieve a result. It looks to the result more than the cause. In English, *why* does not point clearly in one direction or the other, but the response points back to the cause more than forward to the effect. Why did you do X? I did it *because* ... For sure, you can say I did it *because* I wanted to achieve XYZ result. But the word has a tilt: *Why* did you do it? I did it *because* ... the *cause be's* ... So why do we rescue? Some why questions can't be answered looking to the future. We may rescue because we were raised with a sense of honor. We don't leave our dead on the battlefield, and for God's sake we will not let helpless people die alone. What do you expect to accomplish? I don't know; I do care, but don't know. I act in fidelity; the future belongs to God. Although I ask him for some results, and I am very interested, the results may not be any of my business.

Sometimes, if you demand to know the effect before you act, the results will be zero because you won't act at all. *For what* do you act? Maybe I can't answer that satisfactorily. *What be's the cause* of your action? Now, that's a question with clear answers written all through the universe since the beginning of time: gratitude, fidelity, solidarity, honor, hope ...

Recall the advice of Mother Teresa: "God has not called me to be successful; He has called me to be faithful."

Recall a prayer from St. Ignatius of Loyola: "Teach me, O Lord, to do thy will – to give and not to count the cost – to fight and not to heed the wounds – to toil and not to ask for rest – to labor and not to ask for any reward except that of knowing that I do thy will, O God."

Hold on. Keep your eyes on the prize.

EK: John, even as I write this, I still find myself daunted by what nonviolence appears to demand of me under the FACE Act. Do I really have to risk being convicted of a felony and serving up to ten years? Must I be willing to sacrifice this much?

> JCOK: Gandhi tells us, "just as one must learn the art of killing in the training for violence, one must learn the art of dying in the training for non-violence." And, "the art of dying... consists in facing death cheerfully in performance of one's duty." And, "the gospel of nonviolence can only be spread through believers dying for the cause."

EK: So are you saying I have to be willing to sacrifice everything, up to my own life? That's a hard pill to swallow.

> JCOK: Everything except your honor. I urge you to consider, what are you willing to sacrifice to save someone else's life? Again, the world asks us, what are these embryos and fetuses worth to you? And you get the honor of answering.

EK: But how do I know it's worth the risk?

> JCOK: You don't get to know. I brought up Joe Wall to show that you may not know if you saved a life, and that's okay. The goal of rescue isn't to save lives; it's to stay with the babies, in solidarity, for as long and far as possible before they

are slaughtered. And as Carol Crossed's story illustrates, while you may have to commit to this risk alone, your sacrifice encourages others to act.

EK: You're right. We witness them by staying with them, with-nessing. The babies deserve to have someone show up for them in their last moments.

JCOK: Yes, as Mary and Mary Magdalene showed up for Jesus in His last moment.

EK: I believe this, but I'm still struggling. It seems like I'll have to put my future on hold. I'll have to arrange my life to accommodate a potentially lengthy prison sentence. And then, what will I do afterwards with my criminal record?

JCOK: It's a hard ask being made. Individuals should pray about it before deciding. But remember, it is normal, even expected, in the course of a nonviolent revolution to see a harsh increase in penalties before we begin to see relationships change, and power transferred – before others encounter our preborn brothers and sisters as people.

EK: And I believe nonviolence alone holds the power to change hearts in this way. I'm still wrestling internally about the cost. But I want to do my duty as a sibling to preborn people, because I love them. I think love has to be enough.

In general

Run for the light! When you are worried about losing control, or about your terrible errors, or about scandal, or about anything that tempts you to run and hide – then go ahead and run, but run to un-hide! The Lord works in light; hell loves the dark.

Satyagraha (clinging to the Truth, nonviolence) includes candor. Be up front about mistakes – your own especially, but also others. This freedom to learn from mistakes, as a community, depends on the rules agreed upon ahead of time.

I [JCOK] asked my friend Mubarak Awad (Palestinian peace activist) how he felt about a man who followed him in a demonstration – and got shot dead in the street. Mubarak said, "He didn't follow me. I trained him so he could follow his own conscience."

Candor matters! The truth is solid solid solid gold – you can almost say that just plain truth is just plain God. Things go wrong, we all screw up, in fact we all sin, but Christians and rescuers can handle anything at all, especially when the group has habits of candor and forgiveness. Recall the words of Fr. Vince Fitzpatrick: "I am not surprised to hear about your sins. It is a dogma of the Catholic faith that you have sinned."

Forgive everyone you can think of. Moms, cops, abortionists, staff, loudmouths, dumb-bunny friends, yourself, God who made the world, everyone. Forgiveness is a major muscle group; exercise it! It's hard – almost impossible – to be candid if your community is not forgiving.

A vision for affinity

In their analysis of the anti-abortion rescue movement of the 70s-90s, James Risen and Judy Thomas identify a key error in John Cavanaugh-O'Keefe's strategy: he was not discerning enough in who he let join his rescue actions, and this enabled violent saboteurs. Among other stressors (such as recovery of abortion victim bodies), this put an end to the original wave of sit-in rescues.

EK: Sorry for calling you out like that, John.

JCOK: No, no, I am delighted. Sort of.

John had everyone sign pledges of nonviolence. And he generally trusted everyone who participated. But he didn't really *know* all of them, and he was not known to them. To avoid this fatal flaw in the new rescue movement, I [EK] humbly propose that we adopt a tactic from leftist movements: affinity groups.

Affinity groups are basically groups of friends that do actions together; in this case, that rescue together. Members of an affinity group are often referred to as *comrades*. Ideally, they all have a history with one another, or at least one other member of the group can vouch for their character on a personal level. Be judicious! Generally, groups should have more than five but no more than fifteen members for the sake of efficacy. Strangers *may* join, but out of safety should be screened for a serious life commitment to nonviolence. They must forge their bonds to the group through the fire of training. By the time the rescue takes place, no one should be a stranger any longer. Everyone should be aware of each other's strengths and weaknesses, quirks and triggers, egos and shadows. You should know and be known to your comrades. You should share a loyalty and trust with them that you would normally reserve for your tribe. Tight-knit is an understatement; bonded in blood is not literal, but closer to the desired dynamic.

For example, in the Black Lives Matter Movement, I was in an affinity group of bike marshals named after a certain occupation, and many of our codenames were edible. We knew each other from college, and after each action we would make sure everyone returned to a safe house. Together, we trained other affinity groups of marshals. Outside of actions, we held picnics to foster a sense of community among our comrades. We took care of each other.

Affinity groups are internally sabotage-resistant because of their unity, and externally they make up the individual units of ungovernable movements. They are decentralized, yet synergized. Their power structures are horizontal; there are no "leaders," but each affinity group serves an essential function, and comrades within the groups have integrated individual roles. Because they are leaderless, there is no central organizing entity which authorities can arrest to break up the movement as a whole. Rescue will function as a viral idea, and you can't arrest an idea.

Each group is empowered to act autonomously, while considering the good of the collective. They are hyper-local so they know their terrain, yet are harmonized with the greater movement. Because they are small, they can be formed spontaneously and participate in a mass distributed action independently. A distributed action is a protest where geographically dispersed participants repeat a simple action: in this case, enter an abortion facility and either A) hand out roses or B) sit down. As more and more groups form, rescue will gain visibility, leading to virality. Affinity groups are the framework of an organic zeitgeist of nonviolent action.

Roles within affinity groups include, and are not limited to: facilitator, scout, trainer, point person, groups liaison, action participants, spokesperson, police liaison, action support, jail support, action support person, jail support person, and court support person. There's plenty of literature on the internet that details specifics of how to prepare for these roles plus more; do your research with due diligence!

So, I encourage you to go out with your closest comrades and get arrested for noncooperation with abortion violence and civil disobedience in solidarity with preborn people.

(In recent years, conspiracy laws have been used in novel ways, and it's possible that this call to action will be used against us in court. We are fine with that.)

Lock & block: abandoning nonviolence

Lock & block tactics offer a particularly grave challenge to pro-life nonviolence. Here, the road forks: soul force alone on one road, and soul force plus delaying tactics on the other road. Both paths forward look good. The difference between violence and nonviolence might get clearer farther along the two roads; but right here it's not sharp, not obvious, not crystal clear. Right here, arguing for one choice and against another seems fussy, picky, and bossy. Nonetheless, we are sure that at particular this fork the choice is between the right way and a dead end.

Palestinian nonviolence

By God's grace, I [JCOK] was blessed to spend some time with a great man named Mubarak Awad. He was the Palestinian leader who brought Gandhi to the West Bank and Gaza; he brought Gandhi's teaching, complete and unabridged, and taught all over the West Bank. He was born in Jerusalem, and was five when his father was killed in the 1948 war, the Nakba. He studied abroad, and spent some years in America. In 1983, he returned to Jerusalem and established the Palestinian Centre for the Study of Nonviolence. He taught and led nonviolent action for several years, but when the First Intifada erupted in 1988, he was accused of fomenting violence, and he was expelled in 1989 by the Prime Minister, Yitzhak Shamir. The US Secretary of State, George Schulz, appealed to Shamir to revoke the deportation order, but was refused.

I met Mubarak in the early 1990s, and learned from him. I am ridiculously proud of a footnote in *A Quiet Revolution: The First Palestinian Intifada and Nonviolent Resistance* by Mary Elizabeth King, with a foreword by President Jimmy Carter; the footnote refers to an unpublished manuscript, "Sabr: Nonviolence in Palestine," (Washington, DC 1992) by Mubarak and me. I learned from him, but the key lesson I took was negative; I think he made a terrible mistake, and because he made it, I don't have to do the same.

Awad was serious about nonviolence, but thought it was impossible at that time in that place to inculcate the fundamental ideas and commitments of the discipline. So he opted to teach tactics, intending to teach more later: "Try it, you'll like it." But in practice, this deliberate ambiguity meant that he trained people in methods of resistance and stirred people to action – and then they went on to other methods. When his followers began throwing rocks at tanks, he did not condemn it; he considered it a kind of David and Goliath situation, and he praised the courage of the "children of the stone." And then people whom he had trained turned to violence and joined in armed resistance, the First Intifada. Looking at that with 20/20 hindsight, I judge that it is a huge mistake to teach nonviolent tactics without demanding a disciplined commitment.

Gandhi ended a campaign when his followers slipped into violence. Clear water, with a bucket of feces added, is not clear water anymore; it's polluted water. Violence and nonviolence, mixed together, is violent.

Can we avoid the mistake that Mubarak Awad made?

Lock & block tactics

We want to look carefully at a detail in the proposed renewal of a campaign of nonviolence, which is the heart and soul of a revitalized pro-life movement. Some activists have entered clinics and then used chains and locks to make it harder to remove them, thus buying more time of life for the children there and more time for counselors to offer help to mothers. Lock & block tactics bother us. In fact, we think they are catastrophic. We have a list of questions and considerations.

- What was the impact of lock & block in the 2020 rescue? *It "bought time" for more counseling, but broke any chance of being heard.*
- What does it do? *It delays the killing – but by force.*

- What does it say? *It says: I demand that the killing stop, and I will enforce my demand.*
- What's next? *In the past, what came next was shooting, which delays the killing of children even more.*
- Is it physical force versus soul force? *It depends on secrecy, not candor; it depends on muscle, not soul power or truth force – because you must get inside.*
- What does it say to women? *"I'm weird."*
- What does it say to clinic? *"I demand."*
- Is it shared vulnerability? *No, it's physical force.*
- Is it an appeal to conscience? *No! You can't enforce an appeal to conscience that way.*
- Does it plant seeds of forgiveness? *No, it destroys the tone you want. Look at what people do when they arrive in the clinic.*

The best case for lock & block tactics is simple: it buys more time for counselors to talk to women. True and good. But if that's the measure, what buys *even more* time? After lock & block, what's the next step in our long campaign? We do know an answer, from experience: bombing and assassination.

For the first few steps in a campaign, violence and nonviolence may look similar. But as they proceed, what's really going on gets clearer and clearer. The activists whom Mubarak Awad (the nonviolent leader in Palestine) inspired were angry, of course, but also they hated the Israelis – and they never relinquished that hatred. So their sweet-lil-baby resistance turned into civil war, and now massacres. Are pro-lifers doing the same now?

Frankenstein

One of the weirdest details of the lock stuff is that it suggests you have lost – or never built – the ability to see yourselves as your opponents see you. You don't have a relationship with them. Somehow, you have lost the ability to understand the impact of

Rebuilding Pro-Life Nonviolence – p. 128

looking like Frankenstein's monster, with steel bars protruding from your neck. Craziness like that makes it hard to build a relationship of trust. "Hard": that's a silly joke! It's *impossible* to put on a Halloween costume and pretend you look normal. Hello? Why aren't the "nonviolent" activists engaged in a long list of relationships with pro-choice folks, getting to know them inside and out. I'm pretty sure that if you spend time with pro-choicers, listening to them respectfully, you learn with confidence that being weird isn't helpful. You notice that bars sticking out of your head make conversations with strangers rather difficult and unsuccessful.

If you look like Frankenstein's monster, with a bolt out your head (or neck), you aren't trying to talk to anyone. The decision to kill a child depends on the ability to avoid facing reality, the ability to grasp and hold to distractions. Pro-lifers enter the clinic and say with their bodies that this child is one of us, that it makes sense to devote years and years to defending and cherishing this child. If pro-lifers add: look at the clowns and cartoons, because we have a show for you, the clear witness is lost. Moms don't see love; they see something weird and distant. They don't feel empowered; they feel helpless. They don't want a hug from Frankenstein's monster, who's interrupting. The cops are no longer faced with a spiritual battle and moral dilemma that they can't deal with easily; they are faced with an engineering challenge, that they certainly can handle, although it will require some time and patience.

The cops' dilemma

Lock & block means the cops have to do battle with steel and wits – not their own consciences. Why in the name of God would pro-lifers choose deliberately to shape the struggle that way?

Some years ago, a young lady whom I knew streaked across a football field at halftime. For whatever reason, I was the one who had to help her understand the reaction to that act. What she intended to display was courage, and I agree that she showed guts. But what she was starting to understand, what I pressed her to grasp firmly, was that *no one saw her courage. All they saw was her boobs.* All they would talk about was her boobs. All they would remember was her boobs. The display of courage was a total and complete failure.

Same with the cops and lock & blocks. No matter what you intend when you decide to wear some locks, what they will see and talk about and remember is Frankenstein's monster bolts.

Lock & block makes the cops look good. The cop cutting off a lock was the most attractive and engaging figure on the rescue videos in the trial. The trial in 2023 was generally loaded up with depressing and sordid scenes, but there was an exception. That cop came across as an all-American hero, cutting steel locks off the necks of some women without slicing their throats. He looked careful and compassionate and skillful and patient. Good for him! That was an emotional high point of the trial! Was that helpful in understanding the plight of unborn babies and their moms?

The impact on cops matters, and we must think about it carefully. We want to save children or at least act in solidarity with them in their hour of death, and encourage moms or at least stand in solidarity with them in their time of crisis, and invite the whole community of bystanders to act or stand with us. The police show up first, representatives of the community, authorized and empowered to act in the name of the community. What do we want them to see and understand and do?

In DC, the officer who removed the locks did not have any internal crisis of conscience, at least not anything that showed on his wide open face. He looked innocent and competent and proud and focused; he had an engineering challenge to solve – cut some steel without hurting anyone – and he did it. Hooray?

A trauma-informed movement

Often the people who display the most powerful negative reactions to a pro-life presence have been victims of sexual violence. Their unhealed trauma causes them to have strong instinctual responses to perceived attacks on bodily integrity, mostly beyond their rational control. If we are to have a trauma-informed rescue movement, then we must examine what about a rescue may trigger trauma responses, particularly in sexual assault (SA) survivors.

Imagine attempting to enter an abortion facility with the intention of ending a pregnancy, and you find a cohort of people in your way. Their arms are intertwined, they are holding roses in their hands, and they are singing. What feelings do you imagine coming up for you? Now instead imagine that the cohort is interlocked, not by their arms, but by heavy metal chains around their torsos, PVC pipes on their arms, and thick u-locks around their necks. Did your feelings change?

SA survivors perceive lock & blocks as an assault on their autonomy, rather than an invitation for encounter. For them, the locks are a visual representation of forced restraint, which triggers flashbacks to being restrained during an attack. They feel backed into a corner, threatened, and they will react as if they are being attacked again. Either their nervous systems will go into hyperarousal, causing them to avoid or lash out at the rescuers, or they will drop into hypo-arousal, shutting out all connection.

When we don't look at rescue through a trauma-informed lens, we miss the implications of our designs which deter meaningful encounters with those parents most in need of rescuing. Lock & block comes across as forcing oneself onto another, reminiscent of a rapist. Building a culture of life means ending rape culture too.

Co-passion

Recall your earlier visualization of a lock & block. Did you imagine that you could reach out to those people covered in metal and pipes for help? Did they seem compassionate to your situation?

Now remember your picture of the peaceful rescuers. Did you imagine they could open their arms to you?

Especially in cases of later abortion due to fetal anomaly, the parents feel profoundly alone. They have been convinced that to let their baby die naturally is to prolong their child's suffering and/or to put the mother's body in extra danger. And even if their baby were to survive birth, they are terrified that their child will die hooked to machines, in pain and alone. The world has abandoned them.

Tragic situations like this call for us to stay with the family for as long as we can, as far as we can go. We are called to offer these families compassion – that is, *co*-passion, suffering *with* them. We must reach out to the abandoned in their pain and let them know that we will stay, that they will not suffer death alone. Building a culture of life means building a death-positive culture, where natural death is not a horror that is experienced independently, but a beautiful journey experienced in interdependent community.

Locks and chains are alienating and atomizing. They not only create a psychological barrier, but also a physical barrier to reaching abortion seekers. Lock & blocks do foster solidarity with the babies who are facing abortion, but they don't communicate compassion for the parents. Judge Kollar-Kotelly remarked on this when sentencing the nine defendants from the 2020 rescue trial. The steel force obscured the intent of the rescuers entirely. Anyone who actually knows the nine knows they overflow with compassion – but Kollar-Kotelly called it like she saw it; that is, she looked carefully for compassion, and didn't see it.

Tiananmen Square

In Tiananmen Square in 1989, a man faced a tank. The tanker raced to get around him. The man raced to get in front again. The tanker tried to dodge past. The man raced into the killing zone again. This happened repeatedly – until the tanker decided he could and would kill the brave man. This time, the man dodged. The man failed to stop the tank for long, but his courage inspired the world. Why?

We saw soul force against steel. The man showed the meaning of soul power: moral fortitude, the power of standing in the force of truth, a truth greater than oneself. It wasn't infinite, but it was startlingly effective. The tank won, but not right away.

That's the power we want. But more.

What Gandhi did was to bring people together and use a concentration of this soul power.

Suppose the man had gotten six friends and they had piled rocks in an intersection. That probably would have stopped the tank for longer. The rocks might have been slightly more effective against a tank – but would rocks have been as stirring as the lone individual's courage?

Can you display courage with stones? Must we choose between soul force and stone force? Are stones an addition, or a distraction?

Suppose the man had gotten a bazooka and hidden in a window near the Square and destroyed a tank (then been found and killed). Would that have been a stronger act of resistance? If he stopped a tank, but failed to launch an effective guerrilla war, would we be inspired by his undeniable courage?

Can we display courage and use bazookas? Must we choose between soul force and guns? Are guns an addition, or a replacement?

War has power. Does nonviolence have as much power?

Some people believe that Gandhi and King and John Paul II and Lech Walesa and Corazon Aquino showed clearly, in the world of time and space among the bulks of actual things, that nonviolence can do everything that war can do. If they are right, nonviolence has as much power as nukes – and shifting from a campaign of nonviolence to a guerrilla war is as ignorant as shifting from nukes to BB guns.

Do we believe that a campaign of nonviolence has as much power as nukes – in fact, perhaps, far more? Do we affirm that? Do you?

Gamification

In rescue, we must come off as child-like, for we are embodying the helpless children in the womb and hoping that the violence intended for them will come upon us in their place. We ought to appear docile, exuding an unshakeable inner peace and profoundly open love. Yet when we dress up ourselves with locks and chains, we are no longer child-like; we are childish. Lock & block follows the same internal logic and basic rules as child's play – *How long can I stay here? How many abortions can I delay to earn points? Can I win? Can I cheat?* It turns rescue into a game.

Ultimately, the locks repel others from encountering us as stand-ins for the preborn. We behave and think like children, but we no longer represent them, for babies are peacemakers; we are troublemakers. We toy with our audience, treating our witnesses not as people, but as pawns in our game. The logic of lock & block is dehumanizing and antithetical to nonviolence.

Attractiveness

Appearances matter, and as I [EK] said before, the pro-life movement has an image problem. Blockades reinforced with steel are a cool aesthetic in other movements, but in the context of pro-life nonviolence, they look ridiculous and extreme. The most attractive lock & block I've seen was performed by Father Fidelis alone; it is difficult to replicate his charisma on camera.

Usually, lock & block is not visually appealing; it looks like force. The action logic gets lost within the chains and pipes, so that it's not readily apparent to anyone what the message of the rescue is. We won't sell our message with anesthetic tactics. Further, lock &

block does not visually challenge preconceived narratives of who we are and whom we stand-in for; we look like instigators of violence, rather than disruptors of (false) peace.

Secrecy

Lock & block depends in some part on secrecy. You have to sneak in, and get equipment in, and then use those first moments inside the clinic acting quickly to put all the steel in good order like an efficient engineer. But this sneaking secrecy is the polar opposite of candor and communication! It is not a strange accident that Will Goodman found out after he got inside the clinic that he was part of a lock-and-block event; secrecy often interrupts communication among activists, without hiding much from the police. The police are accustomed to finding out what's really going on; lock & block presents them with an engineering problem and also a problem with interpreting facts. These are both familiar challenges for the cops; lock & block shoves them firmly onto familiar ground, away from a spiritual battle or moral dilemma!

One reason for candor is that nonviolence is supposed to replace the cycle of retaliation with the dynamic of forgiveness. Can you forgive in secrecy? How? What does that mean? Sure, sure: the underlying reality in forgiveness is something that happens in the heart, out of sight; you allow God's spirit to turn your hard heart into something soft and pliable. You connect with the humanity of the other. But nonviolence includes a deliberate effort to take personal events like and forgiveness out of the strictly personal realm into a social and even political realm. How do you do that in secret? Public forgiveness is a tricky thing, subject to a great deal of deception and self-deception. Saying "I forgive you" can be a faux-Christian way to say, "Let's be completely clear about this: I am in the right and you are in the wrong. You are despicable. But I am wonderful and holy." That's a failure! But despite the challenges and risks, public forgiveness can exist, and it matters. A post-abortion mom or couple may find it easier to face what they have done and turn around if a part of the experience of the abortion, an odd nugget in the memory of that day, is the face of a pro-lifer who understood what was happening and opposed it without equivocation, and yet loved the people involved. Don't hide it! An act of solidarity is supposed to touch hearts!

There are systematic problems with secrecy. For example, some activists in other nonviolent movements have engaged in property destruction – including Dan Berrigan. But if you destroy property, and do not stay in sight and explain who you are and what you are doing, you have to pay attention to St. Thomas Aquinas, who teaches that property is an extension of the person. So an assault on property, unless you stand right there and explain, can and will be interpreted – fairly! – as an assault on the owner. I [JCOK] oppose property destruction in a campaign, but I admit that you can make a case for it. However, you can't make a case for it and for secrecy at the same time. Gandhi addresses this as sabotage:

> "Sabotage is a form of violence. People have realized the futility of physical violence but some apparently think that it may be successfully practiced in its modified form as sabotage… terrorism resulted in demoralization."

Destruction – anonymously, at night – cannot be separated from attacking people. Gandhi called it terrorism. If you damage property, people feel personally attacked, and Aquinas supports that conclusion. If you meant to destroy property and not attack the person, you have to explain – which cannot be done in secrecy.

EK: I have a somewhat different case against property destruction.

JCOK: Let's hear it.

EK: Property damage is not deliberate violence; deliberate disregard for the safety of others, born and unborn, is violence. I disapprove of reckless property destruction as it endangers people within proximity, thereby compromising our commitment to nonviolence. Additionally, the effects of destruction stunts mirror that of violence in that they communicate a threat of harm and escalation to the public. Threats of potential violence are not permissible means to our end.

> JCOK: Nor are they consistent with the principles which inform our opposition to abortion violence.

EK: Exactly. As you said, a case can be made for it; the violent maintenance of property is a pillar of power of the abortion industrial complex, after all. But generally, destruction of property is not in alignment with our strategy of nonviolence, nor accepted during a rescue.

Confusion

It seems to me that most people who were involved in or supportive of the rescue in 2020 were and are confused about nonviolence.

There's a direct line from the way lock & block tactics present the struggle to the police to the way attorneys present the case in court. The pro-life testimony in the trial – in the hours that I [JCOK] saw, less than half the trial – was not in any way about solidarity. It was more about cleverness, a contest of wits. There's nothing intrinsically wrong with a contest of wits and ideas; but what was lost was a clear and ringing affirmation that if children die, they should not die alone, that it makes sense to give away a large portion of your life to ensure that if those children died, at least they died surrounded by people who loved them. That simple witness, as straightforward as "Stabat Mater," was lost in a blizzard of technical legal arguments.

I have been perplexed by the reaction of friends outside prison, who are very worried about the prisoners and want to pray for them. *For* them. This isn't stupid or awful – but it's ignorant and mostly a waste of a precious resource. They have accepted an immensely powerful role. We should be asking them to *pray for us*, and we should be praying *with* them.

I [EK] have seen a similarly bewildering response from the secular supporters, who have focused their energies on garnering public sympathy for the "unjust" treatment of the prisoners, attempting to pressure the state to ease their punishment. Their pity is well-intentioned, but misguided and reactionary. It is supposed to be an honor to receive a harsh sentence for doing our duty! Willingness to suffer gives nonviolence power. We shouldn't be resisting the consequences they have earned, begging that they not be served, hoping that we might be spared a similar fate; we should be fostering in ourselves the same endurance, bearing with them, and preparing to submit our freedom in the same way.

This confusion is just like Peter in the Garden. He was ready to fight for the Lord, but Jesus said don't. Peter didn't know what to do next, so he ran. By contrast, Mary stayed, in simplicity and solidarity. Lock & block is not a sword, but it's still force. It's like Peter listening to Jesus and putting down his sword – but then picking up a club. Lock & block doesn't offer solidarity and an appeal to the soul, to our humanity; it makes an offer that women and clinic staff can't refuse – let's talk now, whether you like it or not. It's not a sword, but it's still Peter with a strong metal object, not Mary with an open heart.

We are convinced that our lock & block tactics match the children's stones in Palestine. If we don't stop it, pro-life nonviolence is dead.

The pro-life movement is sputtering, wasting time – until a campaign of nonviolence gets under way. Pro-life nonviolence is scattered and confused, lost in the wilderness, and cannot rebuild until its leaders clean up their act. And cleaning up their act includes rejecting ambiguous tactics.

The choice is not terribly complicated. Will pro-lifers depend on spiritual "weapons" and human connection, or on steel? Is the intent to touch hearts, or to give maximum effective force to our view of what should happen?

But wait, you ask: is it possible to do both? Yes. However, we are struggling to re-launch something fragile and complex, and deliberately adding dubious tactics is foolish.

What's missing?

What does lock & block *replace*? If lock & block happens, what *doesn't* happen?

- Moms see steel, *not soul*.
- Clinic staff sees steel, *not soul*.
- Cops push back against steel, *not soul*.
- Our own speakers talk about force, *not soul*. (Or they complain about maltreatment.)

Pre-abortion counseling must plant seeds of post-abortion counseling. Steel just says no, while soul speaks of love.

Will America ever use nuclear weapons (again), against cities?

For decades, I [JCOK] have been struck by a link between abortion and war that takes a moment to explain. Let me sketch it. This will seem like a distraction at first. Let me review our transgressions of thought, word, deed, and omission, regarding the grave social evil of war.

Transgression in word and act: We have the weapons to do the job – land-based missiles and bombers and sea-launched weapons. We are ready with the hardware. *Check.*

Transgression in mind and heart: We have a policy in place: we won't launch first, but our enemies must understand that we will respond in kind if they attack us first. We will retaliate: do not doubt it. This threat, if credible, reflects a willingness to use our weapons. And our threat is credible. We have the will. *Check.*

Transgression of omission: Will Americans permit a massive slaughter of children and women and other innocent civilians, or will we rise up in horror against such an act in our names? Well, actually, abortion is relevant here: our resistance to massive crimes against humanity has been tested, and the results are clear. We will permit a slaughter. *Check.*

Push the button? What's left before the United States engages in horrifying evil that threatens all human life, commits acts that merit unhesitating and unequivocal condemnation? All that's left is a decision and act from Russia or China or some other adversary, an act that threatens us. The decision about whether we engage in massive evil is not in our hands any more; we delegated that decision to our enemies. We will behave if they behave; but if they choose hell, we concur. *No check yet.*

Wow. Check, check, check, half a check with the final decision to be made by people whom we identify as evil. That's not good, is it?

For decades, I [JCOK] dreamed that pro-lifers would learn and practice and teach a way out of MAD nuclear war trap. I thought pro-lifers would experiment with nonviolence and learn its discipline and its power. I thought we would see how to protect babies *and* empower women: win-win. I thought we would show how nonviolence by individuals can lead a nation to repentance. I thought we would teach all Americans in every community of our society that unearned suffering is somehow redemptive, that the cycle of violence and retribution can be broken, that peace between generations is possible, that life is immensely valuable, that with God's help the boundaries of empathy can be stretched into infinity and eternity. I thought pro-lifers would teach Americans and the world the way out of the nuke trap. We would lead the nation and world to choose life – against the violence of abortion, against the violence of unjust war.

Nah. Mistake. Now now, anyway.

Pro-life activism today is in no way nonviolent.

In our hearts: it is standard to condemn our opponents as hard-hearted and greedy and materialistic – even demonic and Satanic and Communist and Socialist and Democratic (!). We want nothing to do with them. We aren't looking for ways we can cooperate; we will refuse to try a pro-life project if it involves cooperation with pro-aborts.

Right now, there's not a lot of night-time vandalism and bombing and assassination going on. But the proponents of such "effective" tactics are close by.

Catholics begin mass with a confession of sin, admitting that we have sinned in thought, word, deed, and omission. So how about pro-lifers in general?

- Pro-life activists habitually denounce opponents as evil. Harden our hearts: DONE.
- We denounce them in word: DONE.
- We are fierce in our sins of omission, refusing to build relationships: DONE.
- Regarding violence in deed: MIXED record. ...

Pro-lifers today are generally opposed to violence, but we have replaced old alliances with radical followers of Gandhi in the 1980s with new alliances with articulate and determined proponents of Second Amendment rights. Also, pro-lifers in general, along with Evangelicals in general, are supportive of Trump and dismissive of the charge that he inspired a riot to hold to power in 2021. In that protest/visit/riot/event, five people died and 150 cops were injured. It seems to me that if you're okay with Trump's debatable actions and undebatable inaction that day, you have a mixed record on the question of violence.

So are pro-lifers ready to lead the nation out of the nuclear weapons trap? Wow. That's a dumb question, isn't it?

A legalist approach to a spiritual confrontation

Can I prove that lock & block tactics are flatly evil? Of course not.

Dan Berrigan and his friends smashed things. They destroyed draft records, went to prison and thought it over, then came out and dented some missiles.

But even when we agree that we aren't going to argue against Berrigan's work, we still have, at best, some actions that skate along the edge of a campaign of nonviolence. If we assume that the campaign will grow and that there will be some deviations from its core, then lock & block tactics are at or near the core of the movement, slight deviations can lead to serious violence. Especially in the early stages of an effort to rebuild nonviolent action, you can't lead from an extreme edge.

I can't – and won't try – to prove that lock & block tactics are gravely evil. They aren't. But they shift the focus from the child in danger to the pro-life clowns in the waiting room, from love to compulsion, from a soft heart to tempered steel.

Jesus didn't ask Peter to put down his sword and settle for a blockade. Mary got it right: just be there.

What are we doing in a grey area?

The Church carefully and deliberately puts abortion in a global context. So pro-lifers should see ourselves as part of a global effort to build a new culture and civilization. Do we?

Putin wants pro-life support while he wages an unjust (offensive, indiscriminate) war; and he has had some success, has won many admirers in America – with words alone. He didn't stop abortion; he just fussed about it. But some pro-lifers are impressed. And the ruling party in Hungary is explicit in its racist bigoted "pro-life" stance, explicitly linking its anti-immigration stance to its pro-natalist stance – more Hungarian babies, fewer Muslims. This isn't "pro-life; it's white supremacy! And Hungary is the nation within NATO most likely to undermine NATO in its confrontation with Putin. But somehow, again, Hungary's words—not actions, mere words! – about abortion attract pro-life admiration. Austin Ruse (and John Birchers and Eagle Forum and now the Trumpist Republican Party) have labored for years to teach pro-lifers to distrust and oppose the UN, despite the Church's call for a global authority. So: are we with the Church in matters of war, racism, and global authority – or not? Sure, sure – the pro-life movement is not a sectarian Catholic movement – but are pro-lifers and pro-life activists, as an identifiable bloc, aligned *against* the Catholic Church? Actually, the pro-life movement overall has definitely been against the Vatican stance on a list of questions!

We are *not* reliable allies in the Church's long struggle to build a new civilization and culture. When you look at *The Gospel of Life* or at the *Compendium of the Social Doctrine of the Church*, it's clear that pro-lifers support the Church's vision sometimes, but not reliably. So in that context – a global context, with an eye on our most significant allies – I ask again: are we really serious about rebuilding a campaign of nonviolence – with an appeal to steel instead of an outreach heart-to-heart at the core of the campaign?

The Church does explain and does support a long-term global campaign of nonviolence, cooperating with Latinos and Muslims and immigrants and African animists, with a consistent ethic of life and a consistent ethic of hospitality, offering centuries of models for action, and respecting opponents. So much depends on the ability of pro-lifers to rebuild a reliably nonviolent campaign! So why spend time at the ambiguous far edges of the labor, where misunderstandings and deeply destructive errors are nearly inevitable?

Why go back to what's questionable, back to the final ambiguous tactics just before openly lethal violence? Why not go back to the original rock-solid nonviolent foundation? The pro-life movement overall needs clarity from nonviolent leaders. The stakes are high. Why enter a grey area between nonviolence and violence? It's not flatly evil, but is it wise? Let me repeat the question: why go there?

Where does it lead?

Lock & block depends on muscle and steel, and it depends in some part on secrecy. Its attraction is that it seems to buy time; but actually, it *seizes* time by the throat.

Lock & block tactics transform the struggle from soul to steel, transform the preparation from prayer and meditation to steel and pipes, shift the time frame from eternity to hours, shift the relationship between pro-lifers and moms from solidarity to enforcement. Lock & block does in fact make the pro-lifer more vulnerable, not less; but it doesn't look that way, because the pro-lifer makes it much harder for moms to feel free to make a new choice. Lock & block is not a shared vulnerability; it's a weird intrusion that increases her vulnerability.

The steel buys more time for counselors to speak and moms to weigh options. True. But if that's the goal, there are ways to buy a whole lot more time; the lock & block champ, Jim Kopp, showed the next step: suppose the abortionist isn't delayed, but is just plain stopped dead in his tracks? Then you get lots more time! It is not unfair to say that there's an obvious flow from ...

- Jim Kopp locks
- to locks with hardened steel
- to his locks with pipes
- to locks with pipes and tar
- to an effort to maim abortionists
- which risks their lives – and
- did in fact kill Barnett Slepian.

The shift to a steel force has an obvious next step.

The pro-life movement, and pro-life nonviolence within that movement, are at the very beginning of a long struggle. We have to plan now for a long campaign that must expand five or six orders of magnitude. So as we proceed, we have to keep an eye on the next step. And so, for lock & block tactics, what's the next step? Jim Kopp's way again?

Pro-choicers chanted at us, taunting:

> "Bomb by night, pray by day
> that's the anti-choicers' way."

Don't we wish it were false!

Lock & block has an ambience – secrecy and steel – and it also has a history. The pioneer of lock & block, the person who devised one improvement after another, was Jim Kopp. He led pro-lifers to use …

- steel locks
- then steel encasing human flesh in pipes
- then tempered steel and flesh with tar to defeat saws
- and then he moved on to the effort disable a hundred hands of abortion workers, or maybe a thousand thumbs,
- which resulted predictably in the murder of Barnett Slepian,
- followed by two years of equivocation and lies
- seducing thousands of pro-lifers.

Kopp has not turned away from his methods. He said recently that *Dobbs* means he should be released. And he has a following who showed up recently on the Red Rose Rescue online forums – anonymous, and promptly squelched by Laura Geis – but there, recruiting among pro-life activists, offering links and literature. The "Army of God" is an idea that can live without an organization, but for now it has leaders and teachers and inspirational figures.

It is, I suppose, quite possible that I [JCOK] am the dumbest guy in the pro-life movement. I doubt it, but I admit the possibility. But I have tangled with bombers and assassins at least three times without detecting what was going on. I went to jail at Seven Locks in Maryland with Mike Bray, while he was bombing clinics. I went to jail with Jim Kopp, and I admired his insights into recruiting and laughed at his stories. And the Army of God manual has a kind word for me, amidst the praise for Atomic Dog and other "heroes." Further, the manual has a cute'n'clever/catastrophic idea *from me*: I said that if a person wasn't tempted by violence (hundred hands, thousand thumbs), they didn't know what was going on. I promptly added that if they succumbed to the temptation, they would help abortionists more than save lives – but I said it to the wrong people, and I planted seeds that grew. So, as I said, perhaps I am the most gullible of all pro-lifers – but I think not, and so I am amazed by pro-life activists who are sure that the voices and leaders of violence are not hidden among us.

Activists who are not alert to violence in our midst, who are not thinking about how to resist violence carried out by our own, are complicit in the inevitable drift toward violence. Nonviolent activists in other nations with our causes have policed their own successfully; we can do it. But we have to work on it, diligently and intelligently.

Lock & block tactics have an ambience and a history – and a future. In the name of God, friends: don't go there. Don't go near there. And don't let others follow you and then take one more short step.

Proud Boys

How far off are the Proud Boys (or other violent "pro-life" activists)? How many pro-life activists are members? How tightly linked are we to massive anti-government violence, cooperating with men who would be glad to return in force, as leaders, ready for a civil war? Pro-lifers provide them with a rationale for massive violence: that's a "pro-life" contribution to the threat of civil war. "The Democrats have killed 50 million people; let's respond in kind." Is that far-fetched? Debatable. Is it *possible*? Yes, of course! Pro-insurrection recruiters were in court, recruiting, at the trial in 2023! Some pro-lifers are already tipped over the edge into violence, and even the pro-lifers who talk about nonviolence are comfortable in a vague grey area between violence and nonviolence. Already, pro-lifers provide a list of reasons for angry conservative Republicans to resist cops and denounce the FBI and reject the mechanisms of democracy including courts and elections and judges and juries.

EK: But I do all of this, just as an angry liberal leftist.

JCOK: Not the same! You're not doing it to increase support for our convicted criminal former president.

EK: Touché.

Already, we provide a justification for rejecting American law in general.

Father of Murder, Father of Lies

Remember that the abortion clinic bomber Mike Bray and the assassin Jim Kopp deceived pro-lifers, not the FBI. All their secrecy and double talk and codenames and garbage were aimed at building a code of omerta. Pro-lifers, not the FBI, were saying "he didn't do it," then "he said he's innocent" (meaning he did it but it's okay) then "I'm pro-choice about everything except killing babies," and then finally just lying outright. They deceived pro-lifers, not the government.

All the nonsense about secrecy is antithetical to nonviolence. So how did it become standard among activists? A part of that habit came from Jim, and if we want to rebuild a nonviolent movement, we have to stop it. I understand that lock & block isn't lying; they aren't two names for one thing. But in practice, in our past, they have been linked.

The tactic carries the signature of a "pro-life" assassin. We dare not forget that. And I assure you that pro-choice folks remember.

Lock & block depends on steel, not spirit. That is such a huge step backwards! And the next obvious step on that path was also shown by Jim. Steel does delay abortion, and you can make the delay longer. How? Think! You are following Jim Kopp; will you take the next step with him? What path do you want?

Consistent ethic of hospitality

In order to understand pro-life nonviolence, it may be extraordinarily useful in several ways to look at issues of hospitality. At first glance, it seems to be a detour. But when you get into it, startling and useful insights emerge. Consider three links between immigration and the right to life, and then two more specific links between hospitality and pro-life nonviolence.

Immigration and the right to life – link #1: Initiatives to save babies and empower women and encourage couples

I see two ways to protect unborn children that pro-lifers could and should work on. These initiatives can be launched now, with a pro-choice Democratic administration.

One is rebuilding a global consensus that forced abortion is an intolerable evil that must stop. This initiative is pro-life and pro-choice, pro-child and pro-woman. We have worked on this in past decades, and we should do so again. It's hard to measure success: we do not know even whether we have already had some remarkable success, in years past. We don't know whether global pressure pushed the Chinese government to relax their one-child-only population policy, or was neutral and the Chinese made the decision based strictly on internal economic considerations, or even whether global pressure made it harder for the Chinese to relax their policy, because they didn't want to allow any perception that they could ever be pushed around by Westerners and their liberal ideas. We don't know, and I doubt we will ever know. Post hoc propter hoc: that's a logical fallacy. We pushed; they changed; there is no clear evidence of a causal connection. However, it's good to press for justice, and it may work sometimes, whether we know it or not. If a global consensus that forced abortion is wrong had an impact five percent of the time, that might save millions of children annually.

Another pro-life/pro-choice policy that could save hundreds of thousands of children annually is providing assistance for pregnant and postpartum refugees. In very rough figures, the policy could affect two million women couples. A third will abort regardless of outside advice; a third will give birth regardless of external conditions; but a third will make up their minds based in part on the amount of support they get. So let's make sure they get abundant support. This is conceptually simple – and the Biden administration has already moved cautiously and discreetly towards such a policy.

But pro-lifers are not currently interested. One is about foreign babies, not Americans; the other touches on immigration issues. MAGA pro-lifers will ignore foreigners and refugees.

Immigration and the right to life – link #2: Resist eugenics

Eugenics, not pro-choice feminism, is the great ideological driving force behind abortion. The life work of Margaret Sanger was not about contraception and abortion, not exactly. Her work was connecting feminism and eugenics and enabling the eugenics movement to harness the energy of the feminist movement. She did that by promoting what eugenics pioneer Frederick Osborne called "unconscious voluntary selection," persuading poor and "dysgenic" women to self-select their fertility out of the gene pool, using various methods of birth control. So understanding eugenics and population control is not a fringe matter in the struggle to protect unborn children from abortion; it's a fundamental aspect of our work. Our enemy is eugenics, not feminism; feminism was once and will one day be again the key ally in the effort to protect tiny people.

Kathie O'Keefe and I [JCOK] have written extensively about eugenics, but I want to make a single simple point here: the most destructive project of the eugenics movement was population control, driving down the birthrate of people of color around the world by coercive "voluntary unconscious" methods including abortion. And coercive population control measures in non-white nations are supported by restrictive immigration measures in white nations. If women facing depopulation policies in Africa and Asia believe that America and Europe will not welcome them, the pressure on them to accede and abort is much greater.

Further, if I may over-simplify to be quick: the basic argument for restricting immigration is that we cannot afford to help millions and millions of immigrants. But if the richest nation on earth, which has a population density that is much lower than the world average, cannot afford to help new citizens, then the rest of the world – less wealthy, more densely populated – certainly cannot handle a much greater influx. We may feel threatened by population growth via immigration, while they feel threatened by population growth via birth; but if crowding is a reason to restrict immigration, then it's also a reason to restrict births. In other words, the strongest arguments for restricting immigration are also arguments for population control. Pro-lifers who ally themselves with anti-immigration forces cease to be pro-life, and join Planned Parenthood – by accident, perhaps, but still with murderous effect.

Immigration issues are much more closely tied to abortion than matters of sexual expression.

Immigration and the right to life – link #3: Consistent ethic of hospitality

St. John Paul II, in his *Gospel of Life*, is careful to place abortion in the context of other life issues, including war and capital punishment. Putting it this way helps to clarify that we are saying that abortion is about killing people, not about aberrations in sexual behavior. Consistency clarifies.

It seems to me that just as a consistent ethic of life is a powerful teaching approach, so also a consistent ethic of hospitality is too.

When we ask a pregnant woman to choose life, we are asking her to up-end her life, to re-arrange her plans for the next several decades. How can we ask her to do that if we, as a nation, cannot see our way clear to re-arrange our lives in far less pervasive ways in order to help immigrants? In honesty, we can't, can we? We say a woman needs to sacrifice her lifestyle, relationship, body, and future for her unborn child; are we not hypocrites if we're not willing to do the same?

EK: When we risk incarceration from nonviolent action, we prove we are willing to sacrifice the same.

JCOK: You're getting ahead of me!

That's three reasons for connecting abortion and immigration in our thinking and planning. But I want to offer two more reasons for connecting the issues – with an eye or two focused specifically on pro-life *nonviolence*.

Immigration and nonviolence – link #1: Facing the strongest pro-abortion "argument"

Since I started working to protect unborn children in 1972, it has seemed to me that the strongest pro-abortion argument was partially hidden, easy to overlook. (I described it above, but want to review it to show the link to nonviolence.) It's snobbery: "I am not a "pro-lifer" because I will not associate with those disgusting dysgenic ugly awkward pious bleeping bleeps over there." This "argument" cannot be defeated by a careful logical response. However, it can and must be met head on. And the response is not complicated. We have to be or become good friends with our opponents and potential opponents. They must come to know us and respect us. And we have to be proactive about building relationships with people who, from the outset, harbor a strong prejudice against us.

A consistent ethic of life and a consistent ethic of hospitality are ways to open doors to friendship with our opponents.

But more: in a campaign of nonviolence, we look for win-win situations. We are proactive about finding ways to cooperate with our opponents, and to affirm the good things that they do. Working together with pro-choice activists to protect pregnant and postpartum refugees or to resist coercive abortion makes it possible to see and admire many good things in the lives of our opponents. A nonviolent movement has to include – has to *begin with* – respect for our opponents. It would be twisted and weird to use immigration action as a way to lay a foundation for pro-life nonviolence. However, without some kind of interaction with pro-choice people, including some mutual respect, we are not ready to start nonviolent action. Pro-life nonviolence does not require anti-immigration activism first, but it sure helps.

Immigration and nonviolence – link #2: Welcoming the strangest of strangers

I've [JCOK] been looking at strangers in Scripture, and it has been fascinating. There are different kinds of strangers – exiles like Adam and Eve and all their descendants, immigrants like Ruth, wandering migrants like Abraham and Moses, fugitives like Elijah and King David. But there's another complex and immensely important category of aliens – scapegoats. The scapegoat idea shows up in Leviticus: two goats (or sheep) are offered to God to deal with social evils – the "sins of the people." One goat is killed, but the other is loaded up with the sins and driven out into the wilderness.

EK: Are you familiar with the concept of Homo sacer? It's like the scapegoat, but secular. They are the strangers of society.

JCOK: Ah! I am not. Explain.

EK: Homo sacer refers to the concept of a type of being that is human but is not a person, in such a way that it is permissible to kill them for impetuous reasons, yet their lives would not suffice as a sacrificial offering. In other words, that which you may kill but you may not sacrifice.

JCOK: So how do the unborn come into this?

EK: Modern liberalism feigns neutrality on fetal personhood by positioning the unborn as a sort of *Homo sacer* legally. Fetal homicide is illegal not because it kills, but because it violates the pecking order.

JCOK: Right. Homicide is for humans, not for fetuses! Feticide is for fetuses.

EK: Correct. You can't homi-cide fetuses, because that treats them as having sacrificial value. Someone could offer to take their place, which means they must be someones as well.

JCOK: Can't have that!

Jesus, of course, was the Paschal Lamb, sacrificed to atone for our sins. But also, John the Baptist points him out and identifies him as the Lamb of God who takes away the sins of the world; then, after his baptism, he goes into the wilderness to confront and defeat the powers of hell. So he's the Paschal Lamb and also the Levitican scapegoat. Note: this scapegoat is not just an animal; he is also the Suffering Servant of Isaiah. This scapegoat is not a stranger; he comes from the midst of the people. But he takes on alienation and is driven away. This generous and sacrificial decision to become a despised and rejected outsider is salvific for his people – if they allow themselves to accept and affirm their bond with the alien.

When Jesus was crucified, he died. But before that, he was tortured, scourged: an additional horrific event. And before that, he was abandoned in the garden, alone in his mental and spiritual preparation, finishing the work he began at his baptism. He was alienated, then tortured, then killed – 1-2-3. These three escalating steps are distinct, and each matters. The event at Gethsemane is worth considering by itself, even if it is admittedly secondary.

EK: For Christians, the scapegoat is spiritually significant. For everyone else, consider what it would mean to take the place of the alienated Homo sacer.

JCOK: That would treat the unborn as that for which you may sacrifice but you may not kill.

EK: Yes! We must sacrifice for the unborn to prove the law is not neutral. The law has deemed the unborn to be that for which we may not sacrifice, and we ought to have the freedom to sacrifice ourselves for them.

JCOK: Give them liberty or give us death. Metaphorically.

EK: It's a revolutionary idea. Would you take their place?

The role of the scapegoat – or the suffering servant, or the lamb of God who takes away sin – offers a door into various minor little aspects of Christian life such as monastic life, intercessory prayer, solidarity, and nonviolence.

One aspect of nonviolence is accepting the role of the lamb of God. The rejection and violence of abortion is redirected for a moment, and the nonviolent activist gets hit along with the child and the parents. The activist is rejected and tried and convicted and sent into the wilderness. Then, for some period of time, the lamb wrestles with the powers of hell. This is a task fraught with mystery, not necessarily a role for everyone. But it is a critical role!

My point here is that welcoming strangers, offering hospitality, is an immensely rich and complex aspect of Christian life. And deep within the fiery heart of hospitality is the strangest of strangers – the scapegoat, the lamb of God. When you start to understand this aspect of hospitality, you may also come to understand more about the immense and majestic power that we call nonviolence. If you study hospitality, you may come to see how to protect the unborn.

Conclusion

The pro-life movement, after the *Dobbs* decision, is tempted to feel that we are on the right track. But in fact, by every measure available, the movement is in far worse shape now than it was 50 years ago. It is indeed a blessing that *Roe v. Wade* is no longer the law of the land; but its reversal did not mean that unborn children were suddenly and automatically safe. It is indeed a blessing that there are states where surgical abortion is not flaunted in our faces, but that does not mean children in those states are safe, nor that women find social support for life. The children are still killed by medical rather than surgical means, or they are taken across state lines to meet their demise. Moms experience pro-lifers as obstacles to freedom, not as supports in a search for freedom from fear.

The pro-life movement needs to be rebuilt, with a fresh focus on changing lives and hearts with laws to follow, rejecting the old strategy that aimed to change laws with a hope and prayer that hearts change too.

To that end, the new movement must be rebuilt within a larger context – a new civilization of love and culture of life. This new culture does not have to be religious, but it must be built in accord with a serious and systematic commitment to justice and love. The Catholic Church provides such a framework, explained in the *Compendium of the Social Doctrine of the Church*. It offers a challenge to all people of good will to a new commitment to a consistent ethic of life, a consistent ethic of hospitality – a consistent ethic.

The Catholic Church, following the teaching of Jesus Christ, offers a vision of a world at peace – committed to truth, based on justice, motivated by love, breathing the air of freedom. In the 21st century, this vision demands a new vocabulary to explain new insights. And so, to understand peace in our time, the Church speaks of "development" – the development of every individual and all society. And the Church in the modern world speaks of love in a social context as "solidarity."

Rebuilding a pro-life movement in our time, we need a third body of thought with its own vocabulary and its own discipline. In our time, to bring about a change of heart not just for one person but for a society requires disciplined "nonviolence," as taught and practiced by Gandhi and King, as expanded in Poland and the Philippines. We don't need a slogan; we need a committed campaign.

We need a new civilization and culture. To get from here to there, we need a renewal of true nonviolence.

So we bring a critique, hard words for pro-lifers – perhaps an unwelcome stench. But we also offer an honest way forward – with a wide and hope-filled grin.

About the Authors

John Cavanaugh-O'Keefe is best known for his work as an activist, building the nonviolent branch of the pro-life movement. He has been called the "father of the rescue movement" by *Time*, *NY Times Magazine*, Joan Andrews, Joe Scheidler, and others. *LA Times* writer Jim Risen's history of the rescue movement, *Wrath of Angels*, also uses this title. The title is pretty odd, because the real leaders of the rescue movement are mostly women, including Jeanne Miller Gaetano, Dr. Lucy Hancock, Jo McGowan, Joan Andrews, Juli Loesch Wiley, Kathie O'Keefe, ChristyAnne Collins, Monica Migliorino Miller, and others. Still, his writing – especially *No Cheap Solutions* and *Emmanuel, Solidarity: God's Act, Our Response* – influenced activists in the US, Canada, Mexico, Brazil, all over Europe, Philippines, Korea, and Australia.

Cavanaugh-O'Keefe has been arrested 39 times for civil disobedience. He was in the first group that was jailed for pro-life nonviolent action (in Connecticut, 1978). He was among the three organizers of the "We Will Stand Up" campaign, closing all the abortion clinics in eight of the nine cities that Pope John Paul II visited in 1987. He initiated the Tobit Project in 1986-87, taking hundreds of bodies out of dumpsters in the Washington area and providing respectful burials.

He has written extensively about eugenics and population control; see especially *The Roots of Racism and Abortion*. He participated in efforts to resist the population reduction campaigns, particularly in South Africa under the apartheid government, and in Bangladesh; see especially "Deadly Neocolonialism." He supported the work of the Information Project for Africa, which brought feminists and pro-lifers together to resist coercive depopulation measures at the UN population conference in Cairo.

He has written about eugenics and human cloning. When President Clinton established his National Bioethics Advisory Commission (NBAC), Cavanaugh-O'Keefe helped form a grass-roots commission in response – the American Bioethics Advisory Commission (ABAC) and served as the ABAC's first executive director. The first policy question that the Clinton's NBAC addressed was human cloning, and their report has sections on eugenics and dignity that were written in response to input from Cavanaugh-O'Keefe. When the NBAC completed their work and published a report supporting human cloning as long as the clone is destroyed in the embryonic or fetal stage and never reaches adulthood, the ABAC worked with the United States Conference of Catholic Bishops against this "clone-and-kill" proposal.

Throughout his life, Cavanaugh-O'Keefe has worked to cross-fertilize, and to maintain civil dialogue with opponents. He worked with Pro-lifers for Survival, as editor of the group's publication, *P.S.* This ambitious organization brought peace activists and pro-life activists together; their challenging work was later taken over by Cardinal Bernardin. Cavanaugh-O'Keefe was proud to be invited to contribute to the *Women's Studies Encyclopedia*; crossing an ideological divide, he wrote their article explaining the pro-life movement. He worked with a common ground group in the Washington area, bringing pro-life and pro-choice activists together – not to find compromises, but to encourage respect and understanding. His work on eugenics led to a study of immigration in Scripture and Tradition, exploring the teaching about the mandate to "welcome strangers" in *Sign of the Crossing*, and then in a series promoting a "consistent ethic of hospitality."

He and his wife Betsy live in Maryland, where they raised six children and now enjoy 15 grandchildren.

Elise Ketch is best known in the pro-life movement for being interviewed on FOX News about the time the FBI visited her childhood home. Outside of this, she has seen some viral infamy for her zine aptly entitled *A Young, Femme, Gay Leftist Handed You this Pro-Life Zine*. She often volunteers with Progressive Anti-Abortion Uprising and Rainbow Pro-Life Alliance. She contributes guest articles to the blog of Secular Pro-Life and is a member of SPL's philosophy team. Several of her art pieces are published in Rehumanize International's magazine, *Create | Encounter*. In the past she has worked with New Wave Feminists. You can find her on her Instagram, @antipersonhood, as well as on her Tumblr, @secularprolifeconspectus.

Ketch has been arrested twice for civil disobedience, but has yet to be arrested during a rescue. She frequently does opportunity rescues, and she plans to get arrested during a rescue sometime in the near future. In the far future, she hopes to help ignite the next viral wave of abortion rescues.

In 2020, Ketch did tenant organizing with Rent Strike Richmond and served as a bike marshal during the Black Lives Matter protests. In 2021, she demonstrated outside the oral arguments of *Dobbs v. Jackson*. In 2022, she was at the Supreme Court the day *Roe v. Wade* was overturned. In 2023, she participated heavily in the Justice For the Five campaign. In 2024, she has been occupied with protesting the genocide in Palestine. She is a fervent advocate of urban and transportation justice.

Ketch is a queer woman, progressive leftist, illustrator, designer, writer, bicycle mechanic, Jungian personality expert, armchair psychologist, secular ally, and Roman Catholic. She grew up in Northern Virginia. She studied Communication Arts and Product Innovation at Virginia Commonwealth University in Richmond, Virginia. She currently lives outside of Washington, DC with her cat, Patchy, and her many plants.

Works by John Cavanaugh-O'Keefe

Gospel of Life: A Study Guide (American Life League, 1976)

Emmanuel, Solidarity: God's Act, Our Response (2001)

The Roots of Racism and Abortion: An Exploration of Eugenics (2001)

McGivney's Guests – a study of welcoming strangers – a work in progress, including …

- *Strangers: 21 Claims in the Old Testament* (2015) – a study of hospitality in Hebrew Scripture, the Old Testament
- *The Persistent Other* (2016) – a study of hospitality in Christian Scripture, the New Testament
- *The Two Stout Monks Myth* (2020) – a study of hospitality in the Fathers and Scholastics up to Thomas Aquinas
- *Knocking at Haven's Door* (2019) – shifting paradigms of hospitality in Scripture and Tradition
- *Restoring the Works of Mercy* (2019) – contrasting Matthew 25 with the traditional list of works of mercy (following Aquinas)
- Two more parts of the series – studies of American saints and hospitality, then magisterial teaching about hospitality, are started but not yet complete (2024).

The Pope or the Pol: Whose Vision Shapes Us? (2023) – contrasting the hopeful vision of St. John Paul II in *Ecclesia in America* with the dystopian views of Pat Buchanan in *The Death of the West*

Works by Elise Ketch

A Young, Femme, Gay Leftist Handed You this Pro-Life Zine (2022)

Sign of the Crossing
6510 Damascus Rd
Laytonsville, MD 20882

Made in the USA
Middletown, DE
24 September 2024

61427252R00099